MY SON, MY SON

BERT M. FARIAS
DANIEL P. FARIAS

FATHERING AND TRAINING A HOLY GENERATION

CONTENTS

Acknowledgments

I'd like to acknowledge some special people who have had a part in this book project. Of course, my son Daniel's contributions are a major part of this book, and I would like to thank him for his diligence. A more honorable son no man could have.

Commendations also to my darling wife, Carolyn, for her work in selecting the photos and overseeing the full design of the book cover and interior. Daniel is the son of our love.

I'd like to thank my brother, Roy, for his assistance in the first editing of this book, and Janelle Zander, for her excellent work in the final edit. Thanks also to Daniel Clausen of Codex Spiritualis for formatting the book, and Sarah Swan Photography for her cover photos.

Special mention to our dear friend, Diane Tohline; she was an inspiration to us when Daniel was just a toddler as she shared tidbits of wisdom on training children. She and her husband, Jayce, have raised three outstanding children who are now adults.

I'd also like to thank my pastor friend, Tim Schmidt, for his valuable addition to the book, which appears in the final chapter, and the four couples whose testimonies also appear in chapter 11. They share details of the trials they've had with their children. Two of the couples are still fighting the good fight of faith and have chosen to remain anonymous. They have my deepest admiration. The other two, Phil and Dianne Thurmond and Ron and Tammy Bacon, have been named. We are grateful for each of their very touching and hope-filled contributions.

My sincere appreciation to our dear friends and pastors of International Family Church, Jonathan and Verna Del Turco, for writing the foreword to the book, and for all the love and support they've given us throughout the many years of our friendship. Their family's legacy is one of the richest I know.

Finally, this book would not be complete without giving the greatest of honors to my most precious parents, John and Maria Farias. They came to the great country of the United States as immigrants in 1966 in their mid-30s to pioneer a new life on foreign soil. With no English and no education, they toiled long hours in factories and mills, overcoming many obstacles, to create for themselves a new and better life with more opportunities for my brother and me. I am forever indebted to them for the price they paid and the sacrifices they made. Daniel is their only grandson and the crown of their old age.

Foreword

Everybody loves a good story and *My Son, My Son* is the story of a relationship between a father and his son and their journey of life together. What makes this story so special to us is that we know this father and his son personally.

The greatest influence in the life of a child is what happens under the roof of his or her home. Many parents have abdicated the training of their children to the Church, Christian school, day care, coaches and camps. While all of these can positively impact the life of a child, they are not meant to take the place of parents and the training that must take place in the home.

Bert passionately shares, from his heart, how God led him in training his son, Daniel, to be the man of God he is today, while Daniel gives an honest perspective of how he received his training as well as how he processed and overcame some critical moments when his faith was challenged.

There is no greater investment parents can make than by obeying their heavenly mandate to raise godly children to impact their generation. Bert clearly lays out his journey and how God walked him through the training of his son. His instruction to parents is honest and clear and, though all parents differ in their styles of raising children, you will most definitely share a common burden to do your part to see your children become strong in character and enjoy a vital relationship with Jesus Christ.

In the everyday busyness of life, it is easy to lose sight of the purpose of raising children. With the years now passing faster than we can keep up with, it is important to remember that the Lord has a specific game plan for your children to fulfill their destinies and serve their generation.

As pastors with more than 30 years of experience who have witnessed firsthand the crisis families are in today, we would highly recommend *My Son, My Son* as a great tool for churches to use in small groups and as an invaluable resource for parenting workshops.

Verna and I believe that this book will help you focus, give clear instruction, and explain God's mandates in a practical way so that you can begin your pathway of intentional parenting today!

Pastor Jonathan and Verna Del Turco

International Family Church

North Reading, MA

Preface

In the spring of 2013, as my wife, Carolyn, and I were waiting on the Lord together, the Spirit of God highlighted this book to us. He showed us that our son, Daniel, and I were to jointly write it—going back and forth with our unique perspectives and thoughts, including pictures of the distinct seasons of our lives. When we received the Lord's wisdom and direction for this book, excitement was birthed in us, and God's grace was released in Daniel and me to write it.

The Holy Spirit also witnessed to us that this work was to be an inspiration not only to fathers and sons, but to mothers. Of course, the truths and examples within these pages could apply to daughters as well. "*Wise is the man who hearkens to this word and builds his house on this rock,*" He said.

Outside of a miracle of grace, a boy cannot truly become a man without his father's help. And we'll only be true fathers to our children when we are rooted in the Fatherhood of God. Having an only son has given me a stronger identification with God the Father. It has caused me to peer deeper into the heart of Him who also has an only Son, whom He gave up for us all.

As they say, when it comes to child training, prevention is always better than the cure. It is easier for a child to be trained in the ways of the Lord by the example of his parents than to renew his mind later in life with the Word of God.

As young fathers and mothers hearken to this book's message, it is my hope that they will spare themselves unnecessary heartache, grief, and trouble that can come from not nurturing their children in the ways of the Lord. Older parents who have wayward children are not without hope either, as toward the end of the book I've included a chapter especially for them.

I would also like to dedicate this book to the young fatherless generation of our day who grew up in broken homes without the love, security, and affirmation of a father. Many of them will be redeemed, and, by the grace and mercy of God, they will learn to be outstanding fathers. The Lord will be greatly glorified in their fatherhood.

Solomon quotes his father throughout the first nine chapters of Proverbs and in chapter 4 he tells of the love his father and mother had for him: "*When I was my father's son, tender and the only one in the sight of my mother, he also taught me, and said to me: 'Let your heart retain my words; Keep my commands, and live'*" (Prov. 4:3-4).

The "*only one*" in this passage is translated from the Hebrew word *yachid*, which means an "only child," "a precious life" (Gen 22:2; Word Wealth definition for only son; New Spirit Filled Life Bible). It is the same word used to describe Abraham's miracle son, Isaac. Equally noteworthy is that the phrase "His only begotten Son" in John 3:16 in the Hebrew New Testament is the same word: His *yachid*.

Years ago in a hospital delivery room, as I observed my infant son slipping out of his mother's womb and into the world, my heart leapt with an unspeakable joy and a thousand other emotions I could not describe. I remember it like it was yesterday. I knew then my life would never be the same. I was forever joined to a tiny soul who needed me—an eternal spirit whose heart was beating for me to father him, to love him, to listen to him, to play with him, and to just assure him that everything would be all right. Before long he'd have his own thoughts, hopes, and dreams, and very soon he'd be calling me Daddy.

I could hardly wait. Sweet bliss filled my heart!

When my son, Daniel, was born, I knew a love I hadn't known

before.

I knew a life I hadn't known before.

This is the story of that love.

This is the memoir of that life.

This is the journey of a father and his *yachid*.

I hope you enjoy it.

Father-son time.

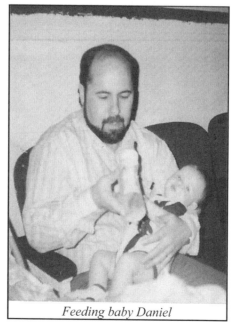

Feeding baby Daniel

Chapter 1
Today You Were Born

One of the greatest joys of life is the birth of a child. Every couple has their story. We have ours. Four years before my son, Daniel, was born, the Spirit of God spoke to me and said, "*Your first child shall be a special treasure and child unto the Lord. He will be a delight to both you and Carolyn, and he will bring a healing to your heart, and will be a wonder to you and even others. He will be a child with keen eyes, and wisdom and understanding shall be the cornerstone of his life*" (dated 4-26-91).

What has God said to you about your children? Each one is unique. Their spirits, personalities, temperaments, gifts, and callings are all different. As the primary caretaker of your children, you are most responsible for how they develop and turn out. Ask God about your children. He will answer you. He will give you wisdom. His word to you will give you a hope and a future for both you and them.

We named our son Daniel because of this word the Lord gave us concerning him. In the Hebrew culture and in the roots of the manner in which we give names to things and children, to name someone is to know his character and nature. Wisdom and understanding were characteristics of the prophet Daniel in the Bible.

We were well into our fourth year of marriage and we had a promise from God that we would have a son, but Carolyn had not yet conceived. We knew the Spirit of God had spoken to us so we continued to hold fast to His word. During this time we were missionaries in Gambia, West Africa. One day while I was at the offices of the Bible school we had founded, our administrator received an urgent call from Carolyn asking me to hurry home. I thought something was terribly wrong, so I rushed home in a panic. But when I arrived, she called me into our bedroom and, with a glow in her eyes, gave me the joyful news. She was pregnant!

God's promise had come to pass. We knew we would have a boy!

About 11 weeks into the pregnancy, however, Carolyn began to have some trouble. She started bleeding and hemorrhaging. The Gambian doctor told us she was threatening to miscarry and advised that she return to America to see if the baby's life could be spared. We were very concerned, and it was painful for me to put her on an aircraft by herself to make the long trip back to the US through Europe—during the end-of-year holiday time, no less. We had just started the Bible school and we decided that I should stay.

When she arrived in the States, she called me and told me how difficult the trip was. They gave her a wheelchair at the airport, but since she was a young woman and seemed perfectly healthy, they accused her of drug smuggling, searched her, and interrogated her. Carolyn cried for three hours. I was furious!

Then later, just hours after she arrived on New Year's Eve, I received the dreaded phone call. Carolyn's mother had rushed her to the hospital in the middle of the night. She had miscarried our baby boy.

Stunned and numb, I contemplated the news, asking myself: *How could this be? I don't understand! God gave us a promise!*

We were both heartbroken as we tried to console each other over the phone. Once I hung up, I closed all the curtains in our Gambian home, no longer desiring to see the sun shine. This was one holiday season in which I could not participate in any festivities. It was dark in my soul. I heard a voice whispering to me, "Happy New Year! This is how much God loves you." Of course, it was the enemy of our souls.

So many questions raced through my mind, but the "Why?" rang the loudest. We had left our home in America to come to West Africa. We had left our Christian culture and were now living in a Muslim land. We had made many sacrifices to get here and live here. We had no known sin in our lives. As far as we knew, we were walking in obedience to God. Why did God allow this to happen?

For the next three weeks we grieved alone in separate parts of the world. Carolyn and I could not comfort nor console one another except by phone. I had no desire to do anything, or see anybody. I could hardly even talk to God.

Our hearts were crushed. We needed God's intervention. We needed to hear from heaven. We needed our hearts mended and healed.

He Heals the Broken-Hearted

The healing the Holy Spirit mentioned in the prophecy at the beginning of this chapter was for the broken heart that Carolyn and I now had. Obviously, when this prophetic word came nearly three years earlier, I had no way of knowing that we would need healing for a broken heart. It was proof of the accuracy of this word.

That healing was a process, which began with revelation from a minister whom we had never met. He spoke the following word to me during a Sunday morning church meeting under a strong anointing of the Holy Spirit approximately three weeks after the miscarriage.

"For your desire for your wife shall be fulfilled, saith the Lord. For no one does My work and goes back a failure, and no one pours out himself, and I leave disappointed, for I shall fulfill your desire, and your joy shall be made full, saith the Lord.

For thus saith the Lord, You shall no more weep in sorrow. You shall no more weep in sorrow. For My joy shall overflow in your insides, saith the Lord, for I shall overwhelm you with My power and My glory.

For a new Spirit shall come upon you, and you shall be careful to follow that Spirit, for that Spirit shall direct you and cause you to do things, and you shall obey, and you shall follow, saith the Lord. I shall anoint a son that shall be born unto you, and he shall walk in your steps."

First steps in Gambia at 9 months.

This prophetic word totally and completely set me free from the grief and depression of having lost our first son. Due to the very personal nature of this word, there was a vibrating resonation in me that seeped down into the deepest recesses of my heart. That is how it is when you receive a Spirit-to-spirit revelatory word from God. I was washed with the glory of the Lord!

Up until that point my heart was broken in pieces, because the child God promised—and whom Carolyn and I longed for, prayed for, and waited for—was gone. We never got to know him. His spirit is in heaven waiting for us. How precious! But now we had another promise from God confirming the first promise that we would indeed have another son. Our hearts received healing and a measure of peace. This word caused new, living hope to spring forth within us.

A little over a year later, when Daniel was finally born, out of my extreme jubilation, I wrote him a letter.

My precious son,

Today you were born. To your mother and me you bring great joy. We are delighted to have you as part of our family and home. Many have prayed for your conception and birth. You are a son of promise and a fulfillment of divine prophecy. Your name is Daniel Paul. Daniel, for the wisdom and understanding that the prophet inherited (Dan. 1:20, 5:14) is also yours, and Paul, because you come to us at a time when your mother and I are missionaries in Africa.

Your mother has carried you for nine months and worked very hard to bring you into this world. We feel that we already know you and that you know us. Your life and presence infuse new hope and strength into our lives. Indeed, you are a blessing from the Lord that makes your mother and me rich.

You come into this world, my son, at a time when there is great wickedness, injustice, and corruption. You are privileged to be born into a godly family and into an eternal inheritance. Your mother and I are responsible to train you and teach you in the ways of the Lord. We will do our very best to make you a champion in life.

My precious son, today you have crowned your daddy's life. I am drunk with ecstasy and tearful emotion because you are with me. I so look forward to sharing the cup of life with you. Together we shall learn of one another and time shall be our friend. Please know, my precious son, that I love you, I love you, I love you.

Your Daddy

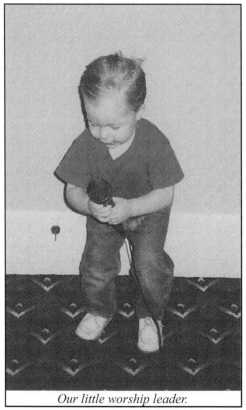

Our little worship leader.

The boy model.

First drums at 20 months.

Chapter 2
Giving Your Child Identity

Daniel was just three to four months old when one day I sat him on my belly with his little body nestled against my knees. I will never forget what happened next.

For 20 minutes or so I spoke to him concerning his life and calling in Christ Jesus. His eyes and my eyes were locked in on each other. There were no distractions. It was spirit-to-spirit communication. I talked. Daniel listened. I was filled with joy at his intent look and focused expressions and started laughing; he laughed with me. We had a time in the Spirit.

Some would doubt that an infant could understand such conversation. Of course, his natural mind could not, but human beings are spirits, and spirits have a much higher capacity to understand and receive spiritual impartation.

Don't underestimate the spirit of a child—or even an infant—to receive spiritual communication like this. Parents must minister to their children's spirits and begin declaring an identity in them from infancy. Purpose plays a key role in establishing a child's identity. Names of children can be important in this regard. An example of this is when the virgin Mary was found with child of the Holy Spirit and the angel told her husband, Joseph, in a dream what to name the child.

"Joseph, son of David, do not be afraid to take to you Mary your wife, for that which is conceived in her is of the Holy Spirit. And she will bring forth a Son, and you shall call His name Jesus, for He will save His people from their sins" (Matt. 1:20-21).

Notice that the name was attached to the purpose of the child.

Actually, the name and purpose were one and the same.

Now granted, the Lord will not speak to every parent in this spectacular way, but you still need to inquire of Him concerning your child. He may not speak to you before he is born or even shortly thereafter, but, at some early point in your child's life, you should expect to receive direction and insight into his character, divine purpose, God-given gifts and destiny. God is faithful. He will reveal things to you if you will ask Him. He may not specifically tell you what to name your child or his life's specific purpose, but He will enlighten you as to your child's calling and God's plan for his life.

Why is this important? Because when a child carries an identity from God, it will create an image in him that will keep him from wandering into darkness. The Bible says: "*As a man thinks in his heart, so is he...*" (Prov. 23:7a). The stronger that God's image is planted in your child's spirit, the more difficult it will be for it to ever be uprooted or stolen from him by identity thieves. He must first identify with Jesus, his Savior and Lord, and then with his life's purpose and calling.

Our children are to be trees of righteousness. But early in their lives they are like tender plants and can easily be uprooted from the soil of their true identity. This is the reason we must keep a careful eye on our children's activities, associations, and environment. The devil wants to steal their true identity and godly purpose.

This Is My Beloved Son

Part of a son's identity is established by the constant love and affirmation the parents give him. The father, especially, is to be a strong affirming voice in his son's life. A father should continually speak to his son's masculinity, courage, and strength. A father should not only correct and discipline his son, but show constant approval and pleasure with him. "*This is My beloved Son in whom I am well pleased*" (Matt. 3:17). When a child is valued and esteemed, his chances are increased a hundredfold to be successful in life.

Fathers are foundation layers. They establish their son's (and their daughter's) identity, value, and worth, so that a child will never question their father's love for them. Without this assurance, sons can grow up hurt, angry, and confused, not knowing who they really are, or where they are going. A father's stamp of approval on his son becomes the foundation of his life, his identity, and his future.

Isn't it interesting that science has discovered that even the sexual identity of the son is created by the father? His seed determines the sex of the child.

A child's identity is shaped at a very young age—the way he sees himself, the way God sees him, the way he views himself in relation to others, his perspective and outlook on life, his expectation of who he can become, and his future place and influence in the world—is all formed early in his life through the establishing of his identity. Fathers are the key. Many fathers have little to no understanding of the vital and indispensable role they play in stamping their signature on their son's identity.

This book is entitled *My Son, My Son* for a reason. Those words mean far more than identifying the gender of your son. There is an impartation of possession and belonging that is communicated through those words. He is not just anybody's son. He is your very own son—bone of your bone, and flesh of your flesh. Your blood runs through his veins.

At a very young age, sons and daughters adore their fathers. They see their dad as a superhero, a faithful provider, and a strong protector. Through their impressionable young eyes you are the image of God to them—a very present help in time of trouble, a savior who can rescue them out of any real or potential danger.

I remember when I was in fifth grade how a bully and his

entourage picked a fight with me at school. How helpless and intimidated I felt when they approached me on the playground! He punched me in the face, but I did not fight back. Knowing, however, that they had to walk past my house after school to get home, I got my dad to come out in the front yard with me and wait for them. A rush of strength and confidence came into me when I stood next to my dad. When I finally saw the bully with his gang, I taunted him and challenged him to fight me right there and then. With my dad standing near, this bully wanted no part of me. This is how most children feel about their fathers.

Children, especially sons, identify themselves through their fathers. Many children are limited because their fathers have never spoken to their identity and defined them. When you identify your son as "my son," or "my precious son," or "my beloved son in whom I am well pleased," or "my son who brings unspeakable joy to my heart," you are putting your own signature of approval and value on them.

How have you defined your children? What do you call them? What adjectives do you use? How often do you affirm them? Their identity and how they see themselves is usually in proportion to the impartation of spoken blessing and love they receive from their fathers.

I know there are a lot of materials available today that deal with self-esteem and self-worth, but I am not a strong proponent of that terminology. The Bible says that the heart is deceitful (Jer. 17:9). Self is deceitful. Jesus taught us to deny ourselves. I feel it is safer and more scriptural to promote God-esteem and God-worth.

As fathers, we need to love and affirm our children, but we also need to teach our children what God says about them, and who they are in Christ. Their esteem and worth is primarily derived from the high price and great sacrifice Jesus paid to save us. Our children must understand God's unconditional love. Their worth and esteem must have its roots in knowing that God loves them just the way they are, and that His love is not based on their performance or behavior. As fathers, our primary responsibility is to exemplify this heart of our heavenly Father toward our children.

We were always careful never to call Daniel derogatory names or have others place negative labels on him. Words greatly affect the identity of our children and shape their future. From a very tender age, careful discretion was exercised in our associations and the people who were allowed "front-row" access into Daniel's life. When we knew that he'd be with people of questionable character who did not embrace biblical standards—as often the case is, because we live in this world—Carolyn or I would be in close proximity to keep tabs on the behavior of others as it would affect Daniel.

For example, one day when Daniel was about six or seven years old, a relative, in a moment of foolish jesting, called him a pervert on the phone. I'm sure they meant no harm by it, but the devil sure did. We were so proud of Daniel when he turned the conversation around and asked the relative if he had Jesus in his heart. Out of the mouth of babes wisdom is often spoken. The Bible says that the sons of the righteous are mighty seed.

"Mighty in the earth is his seed, the generation of the upright is blessed" (Ps. 112:2, Young's Literal Translation).

Speaking of mighty seed, we imparted that scripture into Daniel at a young age as a part of the identity we wanted to establish in him. When he was old enough to have his own email account, we even set up an address with "mighty seed" as his user name. Occasionally we would remind him of his greatness in God, how he was the seed of the righteous man, and how that seed would one day become a mighty tree that would produce more fruit with more mighty seeds.

Because Daniel was a promised son, a fulfillment of divine

prophecy, and our only son, he was extra special to us. As his father, from a very early age I have always referred to him and called him "Sweet Son." This too created an identity in him of being warmly loved and highly esteemed.

Daniel's Perspective: Identity

Every child's positive identity begins with a loving home and a caring environment, both of which I received. Words of affirmation and constant affection were poured into my spirit. Even after being disciplined for something I had done wrong, my dad would always hug me and tell me that he loved me, and that was the reason he was spanking me. Love was the central theme.

I think it was apparent in all aspects of my life—whether home school, home life, social and fun events, sports activities, and church life—that my parents regularly displayed great mercy toward me and held me up as their miracle child. With them, I felt like I was the greatest thing on earth. My father was extremely tender with me. And even when he said things he shouldn't have, or was too hard on me, he asked for my forgiveness every single time.

I saw myself many times as my parents had so declared over my life. For example, the prophecy of me having keen eyes and discernment was undoubtedly confirmed in the way I viewed people. Faces always intrigued me, and I remember being fascinated by people's eyes and their expressions. Still, to this day, I enjoy observing human nature and searching beyond the veil of how people appear to be. There's something that draws me to looking at photographs of people, especially portraits, where I can examine the details of a face close up. I definitely think this became a major trait of who I am.

Wisdom and understanding as the cornerstone of my life were born inside my spirit, just as the Lord had spoken to my Dad. Discernment of good and evil commonly arose in my heart when I was with my parents.

Take, as an example, a story of me and my dad lingering in the waiting area of a TGI Friday's restaurant when I was about nine or ten years old. It was a Friday party night and I could sense in my spirit the sin that was present in that place. One young lady had walked out and said the "f" word. The atmosphere just reeked of iniquity and my innocent inner man could sense it. Being conscious of the difference between right and wrong and possessing a clear understanding of sin and evil became a normal part of my nature.

All of this played a strong role in the development of my identity as it related to my spirit and who God had destined me to be. Several times my parents have told me that I was endowed with an excellent spirit. If that spiritual insight was to remain strong in me, my parents had to safeguard my tender heart from evil things like ungodly television shows, suggestive images of sensual women, nudity, hard violence, and foul language.

So, as I grew up through the years of middle school and high school, I found myself more aware of harmful spiritual factors I witnessed in my peers. Topics such as dating, pre-marital sex, drinking, and using questionable language came to the surface.

I remember one conversation I had with a fellow student and good friend on the phone during my eighth grade year. He was dating an unsaved girl from a public school. I'd heard that she was attractive, yet she was not a believer. In response, I confronted him about it, telling him that first, dating alone was not the best choice in middle school. It could lead to sexual promiscuity and unnecessary emotional garbage from a broken heart. Secondly, I told him that it definitely contradicted the Bible, which asserted that we as believers should not be unequally yoked with unbelievers (2 Cor. 6:14).

The identity that had been slowly shaping in me through my childhood was beginning to show signs of spiritual leadership in my teen years. This carried through even stronger into high school. Public school had awakened me to the rampant sin present in our educational system.

Identity in His Gifts: Music in His Blood

Children are born loaded with unique gifts and talents from God in their spirits. It is part of the responsibility of parents to recognize and identify what those unique gifts and talents might be. The most fulfilled people in life are those who have a strong relationship with the Lord and are exercising their God-given gifts and talents for the glory of God.

When our son, Daniel, was first conceived in Carolyn's womb we began to notice something unusual. Due to the unfortunate miscarriage just months before, we were very watchful and prayerful over this new life. We knew enough not to dwell in fear, as so often happens with women who have miscarriages, but to trust the Lord that Carolyn would carry this new life through to full term. We had a promise from the Lord concerning our son. We never even had second thoughts about the gender of the child. God said it was a son, and that's what we said also.

We noticed, however, that after a few months Carolyn had yet to detect any distinct movement or activity in her womb. We became a little concerned until...bam, ba-boom! Music! Every time Carolyn led praise and worship in our Bible school there was rapid-fire activity in her womb. Daniel's spirit was alive with music! He was sensitive to sounds of praise and worship to God. The activity was so violent in her womb that she would come home from Bible school with black and blue marks on the perimeter of the outside of her womb. At the time we didn't think too much about that kind of activity happening inside her. We just thought it was pretty cool that this child's spirit loved praise and worship.

Shortly after Daniel was born, however, we quickly observed

how music always had a calming effect on him, and how at a very tender age he could sit in the car for hours on long trips, just listening to music. He was the world's greatest baby traveler! We also noticed how he loved to beat on his baby car seat and make sounds to the music he was hearing. Even when music wasn't playing in the car, he'd still beat on his car seat and make noises with his mouth. It seemed as if he always had a beat going on in his head. He had some God-given rhythm on the inside that to us, his parents, was very intriguing.

When our son was a toddler, we decided to feed this apparent love for music and banging by purchasing for him a small little tom-tom drum with two sticks. He quickly outgrew that, so we purchased a JC Penney children's drum set for him. He continued to bang and bang on that one, too. That set didn't last long either so we finally purchased a full adult drum set—complete with a snare drum and cymbals—and with this he began taking drum lessons.

One day Carolyn had a dream. In the dream she saw Daniel playing the piano in an advanced, highly skilled fashion. It was at this time that we really became serious about his music. God was further alerting us to a gift that had continued to develop in our son. It was time to take the next step. We got him started with piano lessons.

In the first couple of weeks of lessons, his teacher said he had no other student like Daniel who could use both hands equally and learn the drills so quickly, much faster than others. He called him a genius. That really encouraged him and he began to take his music more seriously. He had found identity in the gift the Lord had deposited in him from the time he was still in his mother's womb. Glory to God!

A Love for Acting and the Performing Arts

Since Daniel was a little boy he has also loved to pretend and act.

We thought this was only a phase that all children go through—perhaps more so for an only child. When one morning as a small child, he cried oddly at the breakfast table for no apparent reason, we thought something was terribly wrong. It turned out he was just acting. What drama! It was right then and there that we knew this was not the norm. What normal human beings can simply make themselves cry?! Many good actors can't even do that.

Also, Daniel has always been photogenic. No one trained him or taught him how to pose for the camera. He just has a knack for it.

In his junior year of high school, we enrolled him in a Christian training school for actors, singers, and models. This led to him showcasing his talents at a summer convention with 870 other performers, in front of a good number of VIPs in the entertainment industry. It was an invaluable learning experience for him where he received many callbacks and a lot of exposure.

So, in addition to having music in his blood since the womb, we started uncovering these other gifts in him as well. Once we got him started on the drums, then came piano...and then came drama and plays, school concerts and the choir, and voice lessons and vocal exercises.

We recognized all these talents as God's gifts and abilities in Daniel. They were written on the wall plainly for us to see. I had him in sports, where he performed decently, but he did not inherit his daddy's athleticism. It was in the arts where he excelled. He would come off the stage after a performance and tell me that he was on a high. It was such a thrill for him to perform.

Daniel's Childhood Memories

As a little boy, I remember being in church services, hearing my parents minister, and jumping up and down to the praise and worship songs. The music pulsated with the beat of a steady snare drum, a pounding kick drum, a few crashing cymbals, and a hefty dose of a reverbing electric guitar. There was something fun and liberating about being able to lift your hands, close your eyes, and sing with all of your energy directed upwards. I didn't always completely comprehend why I was singing with so much force—so much pure, uninhibited passion. I just thought it was cool. I felt alive.

Since I was musically inclined even at a young age, a beat was always going through my head. I liked to bang on things. Eventually, my parents took notice and bought me my first drum set. If my recollection is correct, it was an all-white, mini set with all the basics included, such as the snare drum, the kick drum, hanging and floor toms, the hi-hat, and a couple of crashing cymbals. I recall eventually breaking it; one too many dents had proven too fatal for its survival.

As a youngster, I spent many hours alone. Because I had no siblings, I always discovered ways in which to entertain myself. The mirror was my go-to. Around the age of five, I really enjoyed listening and jamming out to the Brownsville praise and worship team. On certain occasions, I might turn on some of their stuff and rock and roll to the music on my unweighted keyboard. I liked performing in front of my mirror because I could then view myself, acting out my stunt and enjoying the pleasure of seeing my pretty face contort and deliver all kinds of amusing expressions. It provided me with a sense of acceptance and identity.

A Worship Leader, a Cowboy, and Bibleman

For instance, Lindell Cooley was the praise and worship leader at the Brownsville Revival in Pensacola, Florida through the late 1990s. At the time, I idolized him, imitating every single move he made. He played the keys and usually tampered with one keyboard stacked above another. In videos of the Brownsville praise and worship services, he displayed one particular shenanigan, which significantly impacted my own personal playing style. Every once in a while he would sing a line from a song while playing the lower keyboard. Then, in dramatic fashion, he would drop his head and the upper half of his body below the keyboard so that his face, chest, stomach, and torso disappeared from the scene completely. Actually, I don't think he really did this—I probably just exaggerated it to grander proportions.

Well, with my impressionable spirit, I endeavored to make the same move when I would pretend to play the keys. With straight, flexible, blonde hair that danced with the bobbing and shaking of my head, I would perform on my toy keyboard and jolt my head underneath it, only to bring it back above the keys. I then repeated the motion several times until I broke out into a sweat. I thought it was the coolest thing.

As is the case with many children, I maintained my array of heroes and inspirational figures that I aspired to be. One of these heroes, though not a real life person, included "Little" Joe Cartwright, a character on one of my favorite old television series growing up, the classic western, Bonanza. Due to the privilege of being home schooled, I could finish my schoolwork in time to watch the two o'clock episode of Bonanza every day. Not only did I watch the show, but I also held in my possession the entire cowboy's collection, including a black hat, a red bandana, a handgun with holster, and a rifle. Additionally, I would roll up and place a blanket over the back of one of our couches in the living room, and I would pretend that I was riding a horse with a saddle. With this horse, I possessed the capabilities of hunting down any outlaw in a mad rush of cowboy greatness. Smoothly, I pulled out my handgun, aimed it at the targets resting high up in the hills of Nevada, and fired away as I dodged their incoming bullets.

Furthermore, after winding down from an intense gunfight, I placed my handgun back in its holster, tilted my shiny hat back, and imagined that there was a pretty girl in the room. Little Joe was always going after girls in the show, so I emulated his television example. Joe Cartwright embodied the characteristics of a great cowboy, as he was both a fighter and a lover, doing anything and everything to defend his women. I really liked that a lot. So, I found myself kissing the couch, envisioning that it was a pretty girl's face. Once, while I stayed at my grandparents' home in Southern Massachusetts, I wrapped my arm around a tree and kissed it with every ounce of passion within me. To my chagrin, however, my Vavo (the Portuguese word for grandfather), caught me in the act.

Everything that Little Joe did on Bonanza captivated me. I wanted to be like him, fighting off the bad guys, shooting guns, and winning the girls with my charm. He was Mr. Cool. When he walked into a saloon, with his brown boots clanking down on the floor and his green jacket fitted perfectly onto his chest, I was confident he could beat the living daylights out of anybody in that place. Little Joe also had a fast gun, another characteristic that enthralled me. Every single aspect of his character and of the cowboy life lured me to be a tough guy, a defender of women and children, and a fun-loving fighter. The actor within me longed to be Little Joe.

Just as I admired the likes of Lindell Cooley and Little Joe, I also zealously followed after Bibleman, the Word-emitting, saber-slashing combatant of evil. At the ages of six and seven years old, I owned a plentiful sum of Bibleman movies, each consisting of a different sin portrayed by sinister characters determined to vanquish Bibleman and the spiritual truths he represented. I remember receiving my Bibleman costume, complete with the gold and purple mask, the lightning yellow saber, and the royal purple cape. Oftentimes, I darted around our Florida home with the cape floating gloriously behind me. As many children do, I would put my imagination to use and stave off the powers of darkness such as anger, doubt, fear, and disobedience. It was a fantastical and supernatural adventure that always ended with me crushing the enemies in a dominating fashion. Albeit my exploits were pretend, I reveled in the creative escape that it provided me.

In my home school years, my mom sometimes left me alone to self-direct my own studies. However, this did not always prove to be beneficial due to my propensity for daydreaming. I found that acting out scenarios in my bedroom was extremely exciting for me. There was all this energy inside of me and all this creative spontaneity that rose up out of me. I felt I knew at an early age that I loved acting. I could entertain myself for hours without getting bored. Even when my dad would ask me, "What do you want to be when you grow up?" I told him, "I would like to be an actor." It was this passion and this gift that made me feel that I was good at something. I had a talent that gave me confidence. I never felt this way in athletics. Although I was decent and held my own, I never excelled or stood out with a baseball bat or a basketball in my hands.

Bert: Observe your children and see what they naturally excel at. Pay attention to what they enjoy and what releases energy and fulfillment in them. Identify their passions. We have godly friends whose children display obvious interests and abilities in many different areas. One likes to build things, one likes to make money. Another has great compassion to help people and wants to go to medical school, yet another has tremendous athletic skills with dreams to be a major league baseball player. Help your children discover what the Lord has put inside of them and what they were born to do. We need godly children to grow and mature in their identities and callings. We need them to infiltrate every aspect of our culture and make a difference for Jesus Christ and the advancement of His gospel.

Freshman in high school.

Chapter 3
Into the Lion's Den

It was the first day of school. We had home schooled Daniel during his elementary years, and then enrolled him in a private Christian school during his middle school years. Now, at the direction of the Lord, he was going into public high school.

During the morning of the first day of high school, as I was waiting with Daniel for the school bus to come, many questions raced through my mind. Was this the right choice to send our son to public school? Did we hear the Lord accurately? Was Daniel spiritually strong enough to withstand the peer pressure of the world and other teenagers? Would he be able to relate to his peers and make friends? Would he compromise his strong Christian upbringing to have friends? How would he handle being teased about his faith? How would he handle the spirit of this age, especially during these critical teenage years when vulgar language, drugs, alcohol, and promiscuous sex are rampant?

Like arrows being shot into my mind, the questions kept coming, and all I could do was trust in the Lord with all my heart and lean not to my own understanding (Prov. 3:5). He had directed us to send Daniel to public high school. All of us as a family had peace about it. The Lord told us that he was ready, and that these next four years of high school were to be a significant part of his training.

While waiting for the school bus on that first day of high school, Daniel and I prayed as we often did, and then I blessed him and committed him to the Lord. Then the school bus pulled up. As Daniel crossed the street, my reflective gaze was firmly fixed on him as he walked up to the bus, climbed the steps, and then the door shut behind him. I watched as the bus rolled away from our neighborhood and disappeared around the corner onto the main street.

My heart left me.

I couldn't wait for him to come home.

I remember feeling a knot in the pit of my stomach. I had just sent Daniel, my only begotten son, tender, innocent, and without guile, into the lion's den. We had trained him for this moment, and for these years. Now it was time for the training to be put to the test.

Would it produce?

Daniel's Perspective: The First Few Weeks in the Lion's Den

As "Daddy" (as I call him) drove up to the end of the winding road leading out into the main street, I felt like a fish out of water, trying to breathe in the air. Butterflies floated around in my stomach and I knew I could not look back. It was my first day of public school, the first time I would be out from under the comfort of my parents' home in a very worldly environment. When I ascended the bus steps, I quickly realized that I would be the first student boarding the bus that day.

At 6:15 in the morning, this whole public school thing didn't quite make sense. The brown, leather seats were cold and harsh as I sat near the back of the bus—but not all the way to the back because I knew that the really "bad" kids would be sitting there. As the early September morning made the temperatures fluctuate between summer warmth and autumn chills, it also reflected the way I felt on the inside, like I was trying to find my balance on a rope. Then more people packed the bus and everything felt so strange. I had decided, as a matter of what seemed like self-defense rather than actual desire, to bring my orange, New Testament pocket Bible to read as an attempt to muffle out the sounds of fbombs and rap lyrics about people having sex. All that I had learned at home was already beginning to be put to the test.

A new world opened up to me when I entered into public high school. I was a 14-year-old freshman wanting to make a difference, but I was not quite sure how I would handle it.

From the very first day I hopped on that school bus, I encountered an atmosphere that was pervaded with drugs and sexual promiscuity. Although I had seen these things on television and heard about them elsewhere, I witnessed them for the first time with my own eyes. I knew I was different because, unlike most of my peers, I had been taught the love of God, had tasted of the goodness of God, and had experienced the power of God my entire life. Now, in a world so divergent from mine, I was forced into an inevitable decision; I could either give in to the atmosphere around me and forsake my values, or I could conquer my fears, and live out my convictions.

My first few months at school felt so abnormal. I could not articulate at that time what it was I felt. Everything seemed like a dream, so surreal. In October, I got into my first real confrontation about my Christianity. I had begun spreading the word about God, and preaching to my peers their need for Christ. At the same time I was witnessing, the whole atmosphere of public school generated a feeling of social awkwardness, and social unrest, which made me feel even more isolated. Walking up to someone who didn't believe in Christ, who cussed, drank, smoked, partied, was sexually active, and obviously demonstrated a lack of kindness and concern, generated tension and conflict within my own heart. But there was something pulling me, something dragging me to the edge, the edge of shining my light in the darkness, and countering their mockery with the boldness of God, the boldness of a lion.

One day my entire world changed. I walked into the cafeteria, sat by a few potheads, and after hearing about their desire for marijuana legalization, decided to turn the conversation in a whole new direction by introducing the concept of God to them. I don't directly remember what we talked about, but I wanted to challenge them on their way of life. One kid had the words "Hollywood Undead" on his shirt, the name of a band. I actually remember telling him that he was, in fact, dead on the inside, and that it was Christ who could bring him to life. At lunch the next day, that kid set up a debate between me and another student who didn't believe in God.

We had just entered the discussion when a student listening on the side interrupted. I had previous encounters with him earlier that day and during the week. He knew what I stood for. Next thing you know, he was spewing out profane remarks at me, calling me a "faggot" and "homo." I eventually got in his face and told him to stop, and that if he didn't, he was going to get hurt. I yelled, "Praise Jesus!" in his face and was infuriated, livid at what he called me, how he had mocked my God, and my deepest convictions. I felt like beating his face into the ground and smashing him like a pumpkin into pieces. The entire cafeteria heard me when I screamed those words, "Praise Jesus!" and I felt like another man, like something had come up out of me that I had never known existed before. I had stood up for something, held my ground, and not backed down.

A teacher came over to see what the yelling was all about. I told him that I had been in a conversation about God with another student, but that this student had interrupted and made an attack on me. Well, my only response was to defend myself. That's what I told the teacher. Then, the student who had set up the debate came over and talked to me privately saying that the kid who I had just stood up to had a bad reputation; he was someone who had stabbed a person, stolen his dad's car, and caused a bloody nose. I could have cared less what the kid had done. I wanted to mash his face in.

When I put my faith in God, all my fears dissipated. Principle came before popularity. Being approved by God and self-approval came before being approved by my peers. As it turned out, just living my life for God left an impact on people in my school. They realized I was different, but it did not bother me. I was not going to back down from my beliefs, but I was going to live my life for God with the same passion that I had given Him my entire life. I knew that Jesus Christ was real because I saw His face and felt His presence in a vision four years before. For me, there was no choice but to serve Him even amidst the peer pressure of public school.

After school on the day of this cafeteria confrontation, on the way to the bus, I overheard this same bully talking to his girlfriend about me as he walked just a few yards in front of me. I challenged him and asked him what he was saying. He mumbled something back. I told him to get to the bus and I said it several times. He never messed with me again.

During this time period, my only escape, my only hope that could be found was in Jesus. Some nights I would lie on the floor or fall on my knees and cry out to God. I would cry out for the lost souls who had never known the love of Jesus, who had never experienced the life-changing power of the Almighty God. Jesus had truly become my best friend, and besides my parents, my only friend.

I treaded up a steady, safe path of self-discovery, an exploration of what Jesus meant to me and how I found my life and overall joy in Him. Jesus became so real to me when I realized that I had been saved, delivered, and set free from the things that so easily ensnared and bound the minds of those who I went to school with. How they lived was the gutter life, pervaded by lustful, debase thoughts and longings, as well as the search for happiness through drug use, promiscuous sex, and alcohol.

Throughout Christian middle school into my freshman year of public high school—just as a vast number of other teens do—I underwent an identity crisis, trying to find myself, spiritually and socially, in a world fraught with insecurity and confusion. But at the current moment, after I had stood my ground in the cafeteria incident and held firmly to my faith in Jesus Christ, a feeling of victory and peace flooded my being. I had just passed the first major test.

Bert's Thoughts: The Seat of Authority

When I heard of this confrontation between Daniel and this other student bully, I rejoiced greatly. It was a major victory. I saw it as an attempt by the devil to unseat Daniel from his God-given authority in his high school. He was there as a living witness representing God and His kingdom. Clearly outnumbered, he was only one among a handful of born-again Christians in the school, and most of them did not provide a strong witness. But Daniel had proven that he alone with God were indeed a clear majority.

The report of this confrontational incident even spread down to the levels of our town's middle school. One eighth grader had heard of it, and told his dad, whom my brother, Roy, had recently led to the Lord and whom I was presently mentoring, "Dad, Daniel is a Jesus freak!" he blurted out. His dad, who was newly baptized in the Holy Spirit and on fire for God, responded by saying, "That's just how I want you to be, son." This eighth grader is now born-again and baptized in the Holy Spirit as a result of both Daniel and I witnessing to this family.

The devil sent a bully to test and undermine Daniel's faith and knock him off his seat of authority. Instead of cowering down and giving place to fear, Daniel rose up and met the challenge. I was very proud of him to put it mildly. To be honest, I came out of my shoes with a shout. What the devil meant for evil God turned around for good. Boldness in the Lord always produces results.

We live in a day of gross darkness where the devil and the world are very bold. We must impart even greater boldness in our children. One of the first scriptures Daniel memorized from an early age was this scripture on boldness:

"The wicked flee when no one pursues, but the righteous are bold as a lion" (Prov. 28:1).

We need to train our children, regardless of their personality or temperament, to walk in their God-given authority with the boldness of the Lord and not to be intimidated by the world. When Daniel entered into high school as a freshman, he was not outgoing but rather quiet and introspective. He was trying to figure it all out; he was learning how to relate to the world and still stand for Jesus Christ. It was socially awkward for him at first because he was so different than other teenagers.

Yet he knew he was being sent to this high school by the Lord. As a family we prayed about it and had a definite witness from the Holy Spirit and great peace about sending him. We prayed with Daniel and instructed him to see the bigger purpose in his first-time enrollment in a public school system. He was not there just to receive an education, but to see his higher calling as a missionary to his high school. In a season of life where there is great peer pressure to conform, we must prepare our children to be champions and ones who make a difference for God.

Avoiding Teenage Apathy

Many professing teenage Christians are dull and indifferent toward the things of God. This has always disturbed me because at this age they are to be the most radical and on fire Christians in the Church. They are impressionable and still being shaped, and are quite engaged in the youth culture, much more so than most adults. Great opportunities to reach their friends and classmates are before them as they attend their schools and are involved in athletics and other extracurricular activities.

Both parents' and pastors' radical faith will convey more to our youth than a multitude of sermons and nice talks. Our message and lifestyle must communicate much more than a faith that is simply nice, does good, and ruffles no feathers. We've got to go beyond being content with only keeping our kids off drugs, free of alcohol, and away from premarital sex. Sadly, many church teenagers possess only a nebulous belief in God, and yet recent statistics show an increase in youth passion to make a difference in the world. I'm sorry to say that the brand of Christianity most teens are taught today does not inspire any passion in them.

Our Lord Jesus Christ raised up young people and equipped them to take over the world. History tells us that the majority of His close disciples were in their late teens and 20s when they followed Jesus. This is the age when young people are looking to discover their destiny and purpose in life. This is the season in their lives when they are primed and susceptible to living radically and sacrificially for a worthy cause. And what are we giving them? A watered down Christianity that portrays God as a moral therapist whose primary goal is to boost their self-esteem.

We think teenagers want ice cream and cookies, but they actually want meat and potatoes. Most teenagers think God simply wants them to feel good about themselves and do good. No wonder our youth are abandoning our churches! And they have every right to.

Daniel's Comments: How I Avoided Apathy

When I entered high school, everything in my life seemed to turn upside down. In saying this, I don't mean to imply that things became worse, or that my life was shaken to the core. To clarify, it was my spiritual hunger leading up to my freshman year that began to stir. One such friendship set me on fire to make a difference in the lives of lost kids.

In middle school I met a kid named Mike. He smoked pot and

screwed around with girls, but I was drawn to him. We lived in the same town, and he came to the Christian school I was attending during his eighth grade year because he'd been having trouble at another school.

He certainly wasn't put together. With an addictive personality and leanings toward darker, deeper sin, I had a lot of compassion on him and longed to see him know Jesus. Inside of him, I believed there existed goodness and an openness to spiritual truth. I had been witnessing to him, telling him of the new birth and what it meant to be born again. He listened.

At one point, I gave him a red mini-book, "I Went to Hell," written by Kenneth E. Hagin. The book recounted the story of Kenneth E. Hagin's near-death experience as a 15-year-old on a bed of sickness. His spirit left his body and he descended into hell three times, only to be pulled back by God in each instance. After coming back up to his bed the third time, he surrendered his life to Jesus. God had saved him from an early death and damnation.

In class, Mike read it intensely one day. Reed, who was a grade below us, mocked him for reading it. Reed was a Christian, but the idea of someone going to hell and coming back, as was implied by the title of the book, made him doubt that it was real. Mike defended himself and the book, and he continued to read it.

I thought that what had just happened between Mike and Reed was so neat. Mike, a sinner, had actually stood up for a book about hell that eventually resulted in a man's surrender to Jesus. Reed, on the other hand, already a Christian, had made fun of Mike for reading that book because of his own disbelief. A sinner possessed more faith than a Christian. *Interesting*, I thought.

Though Mike did not come to know God during that time, nor has he surrendered to God since then, it was my encounter with him that opened my eyes to the emptiness of a life of sin—that those without Christ were truly lost and broken. This revelation played a major role in setting my spirit on fire. The concepts of salvation, freedom from sin, and the new birth came alive within my heart as I witnessed firsthand the life of sinners who were dead to God and fully allured by sin's power. In high school, I saw that they were devoid of the love, joy, and peace of Jesus. The distinct contrast between darkness and light and between sin and righteousness became apparent to me. Thus, it actually became easier to shine my light in the darkness.

During the summer before my freshman year of high school, when I first joined Facebook, I was shocked by the lukewarmness and worldliness of professing Christians. I never understood why people who identified themselves with Christ could watch R-rated movies, especially movies containing nudity, sex scenes, constant sexual innuendos, frequent profanity, and disturbing violence marked with blood and gore. However, the idea of youth leaders and young people in our church youth groups applauding and promoting these films astonished me even more.

In my own youth group, I sensed a great deal of spiritual complacency, and I observed that a majority of our youth did not truly know Jesus. Many of them were consumed with video games, movies, and various forms of entertainment. These were used in my youth group as bait to hook teenagers in, but these games only left teens with an appetite for more of the flesh rather than a desire for God's Word and Spirit. I longed to know Jesus and cultivate my spirit. I valued basking in His presence more than I valued watching movies or television.

In my soul, I yearned to preach the gospel to my peers and witness their spiritual transformation. Oftentimes, my intense desire to save souls drove me to my knees where I would weep endlessly for the students at my school. I would imagine their faces in my mind and God would break my heart for their salvation. I would cry out to God and scream so loudly that my voice would become hoarse for a brief time. If I were to sum up one of the reasons for staying on fire in a public school, it would be encapsulated by my love for sinners and my hunger to see them saved.

Bert: I have thought long and hard about the plight of church youth today. I believe many good youth pastors are in fact hindered because parents are not doing their job. Parents have a great responsibility to train their children by living out their faith in front of them. It is incredibly difficult to effectively train a child in the ways of the Lord when they go home to parents who are consumed with this world. Apathy in the home usually means apathy in the children.

I believe the common thread that gives children a zeal for God, and keeps them from departing from the faith as they move into young adulthood, is a true conversion and a home where the gospel is not peripheral but absolutely central. Each one aids the other.

I recorded the following quote from an online ministry article I read some time ago that was written by Jon Nielson.

"Youth pastors, pray with all your might for true conversion; that is God's work. Equip the saints for the work of the ministry; that is your work. Parents, preach the gospel and live the gospel for your children; our work depends on you."

We use expressions like "he's a pretty good kid" who's really messed up. Or, "he's got a good heart," but he's a nominal Christian. The witness of the Scriptures does not give that kind of wiggle room when it comes to the topic of conversion (1 Cor. 6:9-11, 1 John 2:15-17; 3:9 among many others). The fruit of a changed heart is a changed life. The prince of preachers, Charles H. Spurgeon said it even stronger:

"If you're not interested in the salvation of others, you're not saved yourself. Be sure of that."

True conversion is a glorious miracle wrought by the power of the Holy Spirit. Perhaps this is the real root problem in our church youth today. We work hard trying to produce good kids from the outside in, with various forms of entertainment, social events, exciting adventures and outings. I realize some of these things are useful and certainly have their place, but at the end of the day, have we made them disciples? Have they been thoroughly converted? Perhaps that is where our attention needs to shift.

Then and only then can we send them into the lion's den.

Worshiping at a youth service in Cameroon at 8 years old.

The rapper with a mission!

Chapter 4
The Training

"Train up a child in the way he should go, and when he is old he will not depart from it" (Prov. 22:6).

When Daniel was born we dedicated him to the Lord. Even though the Lord had spoken certain things to us concerning him, we did not yet know what God's plan was for his life. All we knew was that we strongly desired him to fulfill it.

Dedicating your children to the Lord is great, but it is not enough. Receiving prophecies and promises from God about your children is very encouraging, but it is still not enough. As parents, my wife and I were responsible to train him in the ways of the Lord. As devout Christians and followers of Jesus Christ, we understood that the training we gave our son was probably the critical factor in determining the kind of fruit he would produce in his life, and the kind of man he would eventually become. Parental training determines your child's outcome not only in this life, but even more importantly, in the one to come.

That training began from the time Daniel was born. For example, like most infants, at night he would cry. Usually I would get up and bring him to my wife so she could breastfeed him. I was the softie, so every time he would cry I would run to him to make sure his every need was met. Soon, however, my wife noticed a pattern. Every time baby Daniel would cry, someone was right there to comfort him, and that someone was me. His cries were not always hunger cries. Sometimes they were just cries for comfort and wanting to be held. Meanwhile, there were two adults needing their sleep.

Carolyn kept telling me that our baby boy was manipulating me. At first I didn't believe it, and frankly, I thought it was a ridiculous conclusion. "Besides, he's just an infant," I reasoned; "he doesn't know what he's doing. How could he be manipulating me?" But believe it or not, I was conditioning him to get his own way. After I had left my precious little family to return to the mission field in Gambia, West Africa, where we resided at the time, Carolyn trained him to sleep through the night. She would've never been able to do that as long as I was in that house. I would not have let him cry. At times, the cries of a child can be the most manipulating element in his behavior.

"Do not withhold correction from a child, for if you beat him with a rod, he will not die" (Prov. 23:13).

A child may cry like he's going to die, especially when he is being spanked and disciplined; but the Bible assures us that he will not die. We will deal with spanking later in this chapter.

This may seem like a small matter and even humorous, but let me tell you how this sort of behavior in babies and children can cause problems very early in their childhood. Children are manipulators. They will test rules and poke holes in boundaries that you create to see what they can get away with. They will challenge your authority and your enforcement of the standards you've set.

Any form of manipulation is ungodly and will cause an absence of godly peace and order in your home. One of the tactics children will often use to get their own way is not only to cry insincerely but also to pit one parent against another. If a husband and wife are not in agreement as to the training and discipline of their children, their house will be divided (Matt. 12:25), and a house divided will not stand.

At first when Carolyn would deny our son a certain privilege, he would then come to me and ask me the same thing (remember, I was the softie). My response would immediately be: "Did you ask

Momma, and what did she say?" And then I would just agree with her response or, in very rare and unusual cases, I would work to change her mind privately or vice versa. Parents who are easily manipulated by their children, and are always letting them have their own way, are creating a bad pattern of training. They are opening the door to unrest in their home, and to a subtle form of rebellion in their children. Are your children training you, or are you training your children?

It's amazing how many times I've seen children cry at nothing or have a temper tantrum, and the parents just give in to whatever demands the child makes. This is unwise and not the way of the Lord. With every example that you set, you are training your child. Children will always find the weak link in one or both of the parents, and they will work their plan until the parents put their foot down and establish their authority through agreement.

Carolyn and I also avoided speaking to Daniel negatively about one another, especially in moments of disappointment and frustration. We were careful to cover one another's faults and to always place each other in a positive light. Occasionally Daniel would ask Carolyn or me why the other was acting a certain way. In those instances we tried to accentuate the positive traits in each other while covering our weaknesses and shortcomings.

Time, Trust, and Relationship

My wife and I are ministers of the gospel of Jesus Christ. I believe that children of ministers are to be the highest example of godliness among their peers. If we, who have been entrusted with the sacred responsibility of teaching God's Word, are failing in training our own children in His ways, we disqualify ourselves from the ministry (1 Tim. 3:4-5). Now this does not mean that our children will be perfect. It does not mean that they won't make grave mistakes at times and fall short of being a godly example. It just means they won't depart from what they've learned through the training and foundation that parents have set in their lives from a young age (Prov. 22:6).

I have heard too many heartbreaking stories of ministers' children who became shipwrecked in their faith in their older years. Some even turned into skeptics and mockers of the very faith their parents professed. Still a few others, over a long period of time, were reduced to embittered rebels, hardened drug addicts or alcoholics, and a few even committed suicide. That is very troubling to me. The larger part of them just became indifferent toward God and simply co-existed with the world without making any impact for God and for righteousness.

Clearly the will of God was missed in all these cases. I don't blame the children. The Word of God puts the onus on the parents. As I've already stated, outside of a miracle of grace, much of our children's success in the Lord is all wrapped up in the training we give them. Spending quality time with your children and cultivating a deep level of trust and relationship are critical elements if the training is going to produce.

I'm afraid many parents have fallen into a bad habit.

We have put our dependence on the church system, the educational system, and different aspects of the world's system to train our children. We drop them off at school, at the babysitter's house or day care center, at children's church, at youth group or youth camp, at their friends' houses, at sporting events and other extracurricular activities—all while failing to gauge what they are observing, learning, and receiving from their associations in those places.

For too many parents, children can actually become an inconvenience that takes away from their own work, interests, and activities. Parental responsibilities are often neglected because of chasing the world's system of wealth. Of course, we must provide for our family, but not at the expense of consistently training our children in the ways of the Lord.

Parents have got to see that this is their highest calling in life. Through neglect, as the months turn into years, one day we wake up and realize that we don't even know our children because we never developed a real relationship and friendship with them. We never took the time to really listen to them. As they mature into their teenage years and begin thinking for themselves, they confide more in their friends and peers than they do in you because they feel more of a bond with them.

Time should be a friend and not an enemy. Next to our relationship with the Lord and with our spouses, our children should be our highest priority. More than likely they will outlive us and should be standing on our shoulders, doing greater than we have done, and running farther than we have run.

Daniel's Comments

As my greatest spiritual mentor, my dad instructed me pertaining to a wide range of biblical subjects and daily Christian practices, including how to pray or directly communicate with God, how to worship God, how to pray for others, how to hear His voice, how to feed my spirit by meditating and memorizing scripture, how to receive healing in my body, and so much more. The topics of tongues, the difference between spirit, soul, and body, exercising faith in God for provision, and having boldness, speaking the name of Jesus, and witnessing to others were all imparted to me at a young age.

From my understanding, I feel as though God-fearing, Christ-serving parents just naturally expect their kids to follow in their footsteps. However, I found that my relationship with Jesus and my dependence upon God in middle school and high school existed primarily due to my father's direct spiritual training.

To be perfectly frank, I can't remember much of what I learned in the four-walled church building as a child. Everything that I experienced in corporate gatherings essentially transpired as an addition and outflow of the training I had undergone at home. After all, my parents were ministers, and I was their number one disciple. In and of itself, church teaching exerted no great impact on me. It was the experience of being in the presence of a living God that left a mark on me.

I think some parents don't understand that just exposing their children to church and youth groups will not necessarily instill in them a passion for God and a relationship with Jesus Christ. Even hearing sound doctrine and biblical teachings from the pulpit is no guarantee that young people will know God. It will eventually boil down to the one-on-one time you spend with your children.

It is spiritual training and is similar to how you would develop your children's intellect by providing them with a formidable education, or exercising their bodies for the purpose of athletics. In the same fashion, your children should be trained in the Word of God to build up and edify their spirits, increasing their knowledge of the Word, and most significantly, their knowledge in the practical, daily applications of the Word. As I stated earlier, such examples consist of prayer, worship, faith and healing, because all of these topics eventually coalesce into the development of the child's spirit and relationship with Jesus.

If you instruct your children how to pray, then they will actually, literally, and tangibly know how to talk to Jesus just as they would a person in the flesh. The same concept holds true for worship. If your children possess a stable foundation in how to worship their King, this in turn allows them to foster a greater knowledge of God, what He has done for them, and how they can give back to Him in thanksgiving, praise, and honor what has been offered to them in the way of salvation and the sacrifice of Jesus on the cross.

Another note: When raising a child up in the things of the Lord, as my parents so wonderfully did with me, it's crucial to ensure that they don't become overly familiar with the weighty substances of Christianity, such as the cross, the blood of Jesus, His resurrection, and the realities of life after death like heaven and hell. These places are real. If there was a deficiency in my knowledge of heaven and hell growing up, I certainly would not have held to the depth or richness of understanding regarding these real eternal places. Consequently, I would be rendered incapable of communicating to my peers why heaven and hell exist and how the moral choices we make here on earth directly impact our eternal destiny.

Disciplining Your Child

Although this book will certainly serve as a valuable resource for parental training, its purpose is not to be a step-by-step instruction manual, but a story of a father and a son just as the gospels are a story of a Father and His Son. But in this chapter we will include a few practical tips on disciplining your child.

"As many as I love, I reprove and chasten (discipline)..." (Rev. 3:19 - ASV).

"And, ye fathers, provoke not your children to wrath: but nurture them in the chastening and admonition of the Lord" (Eph. 6:4 - ASV).

Other Bible translations use "discipline" or "training" in the place of chastening and "instruction" as a substitute for admonition. We train, discipline, and instruct our children in word and in action. Spanking is a very important part of our discipline, but it is not the only part. Establishing routine and structure, as well as creating and enforcing boundaries and rules in our children's lives is also a part of discipline. Boundaries provide protection and eliminate frustrations in both the parents and the child.

Notice from the above scriptures that the discipline and training is the way we nurture them. Nurturing involves the child's total being—spirit, soul, and body. It is not just establishing rules, structure, and boundaries, and penalizing them when they do wrong. Neither is it just providing for their physical needs; nurturing also involves bolstering them emotionally and shaping their spirits and personalities.

Children need to know that they are loved whether or not they meet your standards. Being too demanding and unreasonable with your children will result in them feeling angry, resentful, unloved, and insecure.

On the other hand, parents can be too lax when it comes to the discipline and training of their children. Without rules and boundaries children are left to themselves. This will cause them to feel unsafe and insecure, and will produce vulnerability in them— the feeling of being raised in a house without walls or doors. Conjointly, when children are left to themselves, they are also more easily bent toward selfishness, and rebellion, and they wind up raising themselves.

Structure and routine brings security, order, and peace into a home and establishes discipline in a child's life. Simple things like making him sit in a high chair every time he eats, sitting him in his baby car seat without him whining and complaining, training him to brush his own teeth at a set time when he is of age, performing other basic functions and doing light chores as they are able, creating a schedule and list of responsibilities for them to do—all these simple routines create security and discipline in a child.

In all of these things, there must be a penalty and certain consequences for any disobedience or rebellion that is revealed in your child. There is no purpose in setting rules and not executing the consequences when those rules are not obeyed. This is the reason spanking is commanded in the scriptures. It establishes a pure heart in children (Prov. 22:15; 20:30).

In the training and instruction we give our children, we must be careful not to provoke them to anger and frustrate them.

"Fathers, do not provoke your children, lest they become discouraged"(Col. 3:21).

If we don't balance our training and instruction with a real nurturing spirit, we will provoke and discourage our children. We provoke our children to discouragement by being too hard or too harsh. When parents are too hard or harsh, they establish unrealistic expectations and discipline their children without any grace, mercy, or understanding. At times children are disciplined by angry, frustrated, and out of control parents. This is really an abuse of parental authority.

God's way is to encourage them, not discourage them; we are to build them up, not tear them down. Our heavenly Father is a lover and an encourager. In order for children to grow normally and function vigorously in life, they need to be loved and nurtured tenderly, with boundaries, yes, but also with enough liberty and latitude that they can feel emotionally secure and spiritually significant.

Here is the wisdom of God revealed in scriptures that speak of using the rod in spanking your child:

"He who spares his rod hates his son, but he who loves him disciplines him promptly"(Prov. 13:24).

"Blows that hurt cleanse away evil, as do stripes the inner depths of the heart"(Prov. 20:30).

"Foolishness is bound up in the heart of a child; the rod of correction will drive it far from him"(Prov. 22:15).

Daniel's Comments

As rays of sunlight glimmered through my bedroom window, I

would wake up every morning and tread to the kitchen. Though I may have been a pretty well behaved child, I had my share of disobediences and disrespectful episodes that usually resulted in me getting disciplined. My dad spanked me many times. But it wasn't the spankings I remembered the most, but what came after the spankings.

Instead of just leaving me alone after I was disciplined, my father always made it a point to tell me why I was being disciplined and that the reason he did spank me was because he loved me. A father who loved his son and wanted him to follow righteousness would not spare the rod, he would say. It was a biblical principle found in Proverbs. So the discipline created in me a holy fear and respect for not only my parents, but also for God.

Being corrected and physically feeling some type of pain was a form of chastising and cleansing, and my moral compass was beginning to take shape and understand the importance of obedience, respect, and honor for my parents and for the Heavenly Father. The chastising also made me regret what I had done, and usually tears of sorrow from the pain of the spankings would stream down my cheeks. I didn't like it, but as a sweeping feeling of remorse would turn and spin in my stomach, I sincerely hated what I had done.

The shame and the nagging, gnawing feeling eating away in the pit of my stomach caused me to turn from the sins of disobedience and dishonor. It was the initial bad, troublesome feeling that brought about the positive, obedient results next time. The fear of the Lord was working in me.

Spanking is Training Your Child's Heart to Obey God

Once again, the purpose of discipline is a pure heart. It is in the heart of a child where foolishness is bound, and where sin can fester and grow. It is also in the heart where stubbornness and rebellion can root itself. Once you drive out stubbornness and rebellion from your child, the rest of the training is much easier. It shouldn't take many spanking sessions to create a pure heart in your child.

The world no longer believes in spanking children. Psychologists and so-called social experts equate spanking with child abuse. Even Christians have bought into this philosophical lie and use time-outs and grounding as an alternative form of discipline instead of the rod. But what do the above scriptures tell us? Are you going to follow God's wisdom or the world's wisdom? I don't believe grounding or time-outs is a godly form of discipline.

God does not discipline us by withholding or removing blessings in order to punish us for our sins. He doesn't hold your sin over your head for a week or even an hour as a reminder. Paying for the price of your sins is inconsistent with the message of salvation by grace where Jesus paid for all our sins.

When we sin God's main interest is in bringing conviction and correction that produces genuine repentance, resulting in forgiveness, acceptance, and restored fellowship. Grounding, and to a lesser degree time-outs, have their roots in legalism by making you pay for your sins. This form of discipline breeds sin-consciousness. The only time the Lord will withhold blessings and privileges from you is to protect you until you mature and are able to handle them responsibly.

A pure heart is one who delights in obedience. The real test comes after removing external restraints from your child's life. Will he still obey his heart? I believe he will if he's been trained to listen to his heart and not his flesh. Training your children to listen to and obey their hearts will train them to listen to and obey the Lord.

This is the entire purpose of training our children.

There is a right way and a wrong way to discipline your children using the rod of correction. Here are some guidelines for spanking your children:

1. **Never use your bare hand or foot to paddle your child.** Your hand is for loving, blessing, and helping your child in other ways. There's a reason God instructs parents to use the rod of correction.

2. **Never use the rod in anger or frustration.** You will impart that same frustration and anger to your child when it is administered with a wrong spirit and attitude. Right words spoken with a wrong attitude harm your child more than help thim. It will breed fear and resentment in your child's heart instead of love and purity. If you're angry or frustrated, go for a short walk or take a break. Once you've cooled down you can then administer the spanking in love and gentleness. If you spank your child in anger it will breed the same in him.

3. **Never spank your child if he doesn't know or understand why he is being spanked.** In other words, you have no right to enforce boundaries and rules that have not been clearly established. This will frustrate and confuse your child. You cannot establish rules after the offense. If your child doesn't know it was wrong, you shouldn't discipline him for it. Give him time to adjust to new rules and guidelines. You don't spank him for child-like behavior, accidents, or ignorance of a rule on his part. Be gracious. Be patient. It takes a little time to train a child's spirit. I find that parents often need more training than their children in administering proper, consistent discipline. A pure heart is what you are after.

4. **Never use the rod of correction on your child until you've sown ten times more praise, affection, love, and acceptance than you do the rod.** Too many rules, too many narrow boundaries, and too much structure without an overabundance of praise, affection, love, and acceptance will produce rebellion and discouragement in the child.

Do's

1. **Get the paddle and speak to your child about his misconduct**

or lack of obedience in a certain area. If he is guilty then encourage him to confess his sin verbally. No forgiveness without confession (1 John 1:9).

2. **Cover the scriptures that deal with his sin.** One scripture we frequently used was Ephesians 6:1-3. "*Children, obey your parents in the Lord, for this is right. Honor your father and mother, which is the first commandment with promise: that it may be well with you and you may live long on the earth.*" We had Daniel memorize it so he knew it.

3. **Explain to him the reason you are administering the spanking.** Tell him that you are under God's authority, and you are obeying His instructions. Affirm your love for him.

4. **Spank him on the bottom, medium hard, based on his temperament.** Strong-willed children may need a stronger blow, and adjust the spanking to whether or not it was a first time, second time, or more frequent offense. You may spank him more than once according to the severity of his infraction. Put him in a good position, either over your lap or knee, depending on their age, or have them bend over. We did the latter with Daniel, but because he often squirmed, I missed him at times and nearly hurt him—so be careful not to bruise him or injure him. Remember though, no pain usually means no gain.

5. **Spank him right away after the infraction.** A child has a short attention span and may forget what he did hours later. If you are in a public place, wait until you are in private to avoid publicly humiliating him. See spanking as an intimate time between you and your child. It is a time to portray the heart of the heavenly Father to him and build that image into his spirit.

6. **After you have administered the spanking, pray and worship the Father with your child.** Assure him of your love and rejoice with him in the cleansing and restored fellowship. This was often the most spiritual and intimate time of the day with Daniel.

Although I believe the father should be the primary disciplinarian, it is reasonable and practical, due to their different schedules, for both parents to be involved in administering discipline, in the form of spanking, to their children. If it is only one, the child will be more obedient to that one and not honor the other as much. Whoever catches him in any infraction or act of rebellion or disobedience is the one who should administer the spanking. Using the rod is a very important part of training children. Why else would the Word of God give us instruction on it?

Yes, spanking is necessary, but above all, nourish, nourish, and nourish your children. Build them up. Encourage and affirm them. Go nuts when they do well. Go nuts when they try hard. Be gentle, tender, patient, and kind with them. It's not your words of instruction or correction that are being imparted as much as the spirit by which you impart them. Play a lot. Laugh a lot. Let them see your silly side. Your children will never forget it.

In closing this chapter, weigh these words of an aged parent:

If I had my child to raise over again

I'd build self-esteem first and the house later

I'd finger paint more and point the finger less

I would do less correcting and more connecting

I'd take my eyes off my watch and watch with my eyes

I would care to know less and know to care more

I'd take more hikes and fly more kites

I'd stop playing serious and seriously play

I would run through more fields and gaze at more stars

I'd do more hugging and less tugging

I'd see the oak tree in the acorn more often

I would be firm less often and affirm much more

I'd model less about the love of power

And more about the power of love

Now fathers (and mothers), go on and do the same.

Our family on a missionary trip to Holland.

Our first Christmas as a missionary family in Gambia, West Africa.

Our family upon relocating to America.

Chapter 5
The Fear of the Lord

I want to key in on something Daniel wrote in the second chapter, "Giving Your Child Identity." He said, "*Being conscious of the difference between right and wrong and possessing a clear understanding of sin and evil became a normal part of my nature.*" Here he explains it more fully:

Daniel's Comments

The knowledge of good and evil was birthed in me as a youngster. When I was around eight years old, I was on a mission trip with my mom and dad, walking through the Amsterdam airport. We passed by some bars and the smoky scene was illuminated with the neon-lit pub signs. My daddy was next to me, holding my hand. Something felt funny inside me like an eerie sense of misplacement.

The atmosphere in those bars impressed upon me this weight of danger and ill ease. I looked up at my dad, tugged at his pants, and whispered, "There's sin in there, isn't there, Daddy?" There lay an inner voice in my spirit, witnessing to me of the evil in that bar. It was contradictory to the innocence in my soul.

I do know that the concept of sin appeared early on in my life. In kindergarten, I had received a set of toy race cars, minuscule automobiles that I enjoyed playing with. I desired to take them to school with me in order to alleviate some of my boredom and to impress my classmates who also took pleasure in displaying their nifty gadgets and primetime playthings, but my parents had told me I couldn't bring them.

As a response, the notion of sneaking the mini cars to school the next day with me sounded like a whirl of fun. My conscience told me it was wrong, but I thought of how good it would be if I got away with it. I would get to play with the grooviest race car set in the school, dodging police cars and watching the tires spin forward as the engine revved and growled and whistled. I snuck the cars under my pillow the night before. When they were transported from their usual habitat—which lay across the house from my room —to my bed, butterflies raced around in my stomach as the potential threat of being caught was fused with the thrill of possibly getting away with it. Despite that, I don't recall exactly how I toted my delightful cars to the school. I can only visualize in my mind how I ran with them across the dirt in the parking lot. My parents never found out, but deep inside me, I knew it was wrong. I had disobeyed my parents.

Around the age of three, my dad first told me about heaven and hell. But it was hell that he described more, and it was hell that impressed upon me the greatest sense of urgency in giving my life to Christ.

Bert: How does this consciousness of right and wrong and a clear understanding of sin and evil happen in a child's heart? As I was nearing the end of writing this book I thought long and hard about this aspect of Daniel's nature that seemed to be a part of him from a very early age. What was it that caused him to be so sensitized to sin and evil?

As I began to ponder the message in the content of this book, I kept noting that this was a common thread that ran throughout the fabric of these pages. In my heart I knew there was a key component in this father and son story that the Holy Spirit wanted to highlight. I had a witness on the inside of me that told me that all child training was rooted in this one theme. I also knew that it was the key to Jesus' relationship with the Father. The Holy Spirit kept drawing my attention to this, and I knew this book would not be complete without it. What was it?

Then one day I saw it. The light came on. There it was in plain sight right in front of me. It's a wonder I did not see it sooner.

The Bible says: "*The fear of the Lord is to hate evil...*" (Prov. 8:13).

That was it! The fear of the Lord had been planted and cultivated in Daniel's heart from an early age. This is so simple I almost missed it.

For this reason I have included this chapter on the fear of the Lord. There is not a more important aspect to develop in your children than this one. I believe it has been the main key to Daniel's growth and maturity in the Lord. It is the anchor that secures the ship. It is the rudder that steers the ship.

The wholesome fear of the Lord is to be the governing factor of every human being's life on earth. It is what separates us from the world and unto God. As far back as in the days of Moses, God commanded Israel's fathers to teach their children the fear of the Lord.

"*Only take heed to yourself, and diligently keep yourself, lest you forget the things your eyes have seen, and lest they depart from your heart all the days of your life. And teach them to your children and your grandchildren, especially concerning the day you stood before the Lord your God in Horeb, when the Lord said to me, 'Gather the people to Me, and I will let them hear My words, that they may learn to fear Me all the days they live on the earth, and that they may teach their children'*" (Deut. 4:9-10).

Wisdom and Understanding

Back in the beginning of this book I shared how the Lord spoke to me about Daniel before he was born. Among other things, He told me that wisdom and understanding would be the cornerstone of his life. A word of wisdom contained in a prophecy like that is often conditional. As parents, Carolyn and I knew we had the responsibility to train our son so that wisdom and understanding could indeed be his portion in life. In other words, we weren't going to be passive with a word like that and just sit back and wait for it to happen. This word did not release us from our responsibility to be proactive in training our son.

The Bible places high value on wisdom and understanding.

"Wisdom is the principal thing; therefore get wisdom; yea, with all thy getting get understanding" (Prov. 4:7, ASV).

Notice through what vehicle wisdom and understanding come.

"The fear of the Lord is the beginning of wisdom; and the knowledge of the Holy One is understanding" (Prov. 9:10).

Wisdom and understanding begin with the fear of the Lord and an intimate knowledge of the Holy One. This facet of the fear of the Lord was without a doubt the most important aspect in the training of our son. It is what separates goody two-shoes children and church-wise children from godly children. It is what keeps the conscience of a child clean and his spirit burning bright. The fear of the Lord is what will make your child wise and keep him from sin and evil all the days of his life.

If you want your children to be wise and full of understanding, you must teach them the fear of the Lord.

"Come, you children, listen to me; I will teach you the fear of the Lord" (Ps. 34:11).

I would encourage you as a parent to cultivate this in your own life as well, or else you will not be able to impart it as effectively to your children. Let the Holy Spirit deal with you about certain areas of your life and conduct where you still flirt with sin and compromise, areas where your flesh still rules you and you have not yielded to the Lordship of Jesus Christ. The fear of the Lord cannot be lightly esteemed, but must be highly valued and treasured. This takes a strong, loving relationship with the Lord where you cringe at the thought of displeasing Him.

"Gather the people together, men and women and little ones, and the stranger who is within your gates, that they may hear and that they may learn to fear the Lord your God and carefully observe all the words of this law, and that their children, who have not known it, may hear and learn to fear the Lord your God as long as you live in the land which you cross the Jordan to possess" (Deut. 31:12-13).

The Lord wanted every family including the stranger among them to learn to fear the Lord so that they could teach their own children the same. The greatest impartations into your life happen through your closest associations. Your close associations will tell me what you have in your home. The closest people in children's lives should be their parents and grandparents. They should be their primary examples and teachers, passing on to them their deep faith and values. This can work positively or negatively. It can work for godliness or for evil.

The great danger today is in the lukewarmness that we are seeing in the church world. Kids have learned to be church-wise without possessing a real intimate knowledge of the Holy One. They act pious in the church but are often very carnal the rest of the time. The reason they are this way is often because their parents are that way. They may even be quick to tell you that they fear and respect the Lord, but it is not the real, holy fear of the Lord. It is a mixture. In actuality, some of them may be full of the ways of the world and serving idols. The sad part is that these parents fail to realize that they are passing their carnal, worldly, and idolatrous lifestyles unto their children and children's children.

"So these nations [vainly] feared the Lord and also served their graven images, as did their children and their children's children. As their fathers did, so do they to this day" (2 Kings 17:41, AMP).

71

Notice these nations feared the Lord in vain because they also served their graven images, and their children and grandchildren imitated them and did the same.

I can tell you as a father that this holy quality of the fear of the Lord is the biggest reason my wife and I have full trust in our son, especially now that he is 1200 miles from home in college. We saw evidence of this holy fear in him at a very young age. One day in a moment of frustration with him, I made the mistake of calling him a backslider. Immediately tears poured forth from his eyes and he began weeping loudly. I felt so bad that I had used that word, not yet fully realizing just how sensitive and tender he was. This was another instance where I had to ask him to forgive me for a poor choice of words. In one sense I was sorry and regretted how I had spoken to him, but in another sense I was so pleased with his response and how broken he was.

It doesn't take a lifetime to learn the fear of the Lord. Jesus learned it at a very young age.

"Therefore the Lord himself will give you a sign: The virgin will conceive and give birth to a son, and will call him Immanuel. He will be eating curds and honey when he knows enough to reject the wrong and choose the right, for before the boy knows enough to reject the wrong and choose the right, the land of the two kings you dread will be laid waste" (Isa. 7:14-16, NIV).

Children can eat butter (or cheese) and honey at a very young age. At the same time Jesus began to eat these things is the time He also learned to refuse evil and choose good. Since the fear of the Lord is to hate evil (Prov. 8:13), Jesus must have started cultivating the fear of the Lord at a very early age. My guess is he would have been one to two years of age.

As Jesus continued to mature in wisdom through the fear of the Lord (Luke 2:40, 52), His discernment between good and evil also grew—to the point where he followed the dictates of His spirit and not His physical senses.

"*His delight is in the fear of the Lord, and He shall not judge by the sight of His eyes, nor decide by the hearing of His ears*" (Isa. 11:3).

Jesus' desire to please the Father was planted in him at an early age. It was the beginning of wisdom and understanding in His life. He learned to judge righteously and not by outward appearance. He learned to see and discern things spiritually as they really were, and not as they appeared to be. He took pleasure in preferring good and doing right, while being repulsed by evil and refusing it.

At 12 years of age, He was found in the temple with teachers of the law discussing things with them, and the scripture tells us that they "*were astonished at His understanding and answers*" (Luke 2:47). His understanding was rooted in the fear of the Lord and the knowledge of the Holy One.

When Jesus' parents questioned Him about His whereabouts, His response reveals volumes of His early maturity. Here was Jesus' response to His anxious parents, "*Why did you seek Me? Did you not know that I must be about My Father's business?*" (Luke 2:49).

This scripture reveals that from a young age Jesus recognized a higher purpose in His life. He was consecrated to the business of His Father. Let's not sell ourselves short of what God can do in our children at a very young age. Set your sights high, and don't say that they are too young to learn the fear of the Lord and to be consecrated to God's purposes.

On our Cameroon mission trip.

Chapter 6
The Power of Example

"For I have given you an example, that you should do as I have done to you" (John 13:15).

"For whatever the Father does, the Son also does in like manner" (John 5:19).

I believe the greatest element in training your children is in the power of the example you set for them. The training you give them will not produce maximum results unless you are the primary example in their lives of that which you teach. Children will do what you *say* when they are under your authority, but after they leave they will usually do what you *have done*. They will do what they have observed in your home and your lives as their parents. Although thorough instruction is to be a vital part of the training and development of your children, it will produce less fruit if you are not a doer of your own instruction.

Seeing is more powerful than hearing. What children hear they will soon forget, but it is what they continually see that they remember. What are your children seeing in your home? What are they seeing in your marriage? What is the example you are setting forth?

I grew up in a strife-filled home full of negativity and it was difficult to break that off my life. My parents loved me but had not yet come to a saving knowledge of Jesus Christ, so they didn't know any better. Renewing my mind with the scriptures and experiencing the presence of the Lord is what set me free from that strife and negativity.

Husbands, how are you treating your wives? Wives, how are you treating your husbands? How are you treating your own parents? How are you treating your relatives, friends, and neighbors? How do you treat strangers and outsiders? You may not be keenly aware of this, but your children are daily witnessing your conduct and conversation with others.

Children often hear their parents' private conversations that they have about other people. Are your conversations godly and edifying, or are they full of gossip, slander, criticism, complaining, and backbiting? The example we set is the critical element in all our training. What are you imparting to your children?

My wife and I were far from perfect, but we endeavored to watch our conduct and conversation around Daniel and to keep things edifying. Very private conversations would almost always be conducted in the privacy of our own bedroom. When we fell short of any righteous standard in the presence of Daniel, we would often apologize to him and explain to him the reason it was wrong— always pointing to scripture and Jesus' words as our standard.

Jesus Christ used the power of His example to train His 12 apostles. He embodied the change He wanted to see in them. He knew the only way to impact them was to first call them to be with Him (Mark 3:14) so they could observe His life and character up close. Jesus' consecration, His love and compassion, His submission to the Father's will, and His deep humility were His greatest examples and constituted a good part of His teaching and instruction to His disciples. Jesus was also the ideal model in prayer and ministry, as well as how He dealt with people from every background and status.

Without being a Christ-like example all your training could be in vain.

Daniel's Comments

My father and mother always seemed to find time to spend with me as a kid. Countless mornings were spent in the tranquility of the presence of God, as my dad and I became enraptured in an intense time in the Word and prayer. I distinctly remember when I first started speaking in tongues. In the darkness of my room with only the lampshade lit, my daddy laid next to me, continually uttering words of an unknown tongue while I listened, opened up my spirit, and became as vulnerable and as exposed as a new-born lamb.

Those first few syllables I spoke in tongues were like a freshness, an oasis of mountain spring water permeating the lifeblood within me. For a period of time my father had taught me, asked me, and probed me about being baptized in the Holy Ghost. There was a brief time where the uncertainty and doubt of actually having the ability to vocalize a few phrases in this new heavenly language caused me a great deal of hesitation and delay.

It was a hesitation, not in the sense that I had doubted my Heavenly Father or my dad, but a hesitation that lay in my own lack of complete acceptance and coming to terms with the baptism of the Holy Ghost. Of course, a six-year-old youngster isn't supposed to know much regarding the profound, weighty substances of divine matters. Yet my spiritual candle—burning with vivid, flaming seeds, my hunger for the super real, extraordinary things of God—was being lit, cradled, and would burgeon with the passing of time.

My parents were undoubtedly my greatest examples throughout my childhood. I never witnessed leanings toward lukewarmness, hyper-spirituality or hypocrisy in them; neither did I see a bent towards compromise or a path towards spiritual passivity. They were the most dedicated human beings I knew; without a doubt they were consecrated to the call of God on their lives and committed to raising their one and only son in the ways of the Lord.

Throughout the course of my childhood years, my parents exhibited much compassion and care for one another in their own relationship. Hardly ever were there harsh words spoken between them, and if I did hear them argue, they never infused foul language into it. They had clean mouths and lived uncompromising lives. Everything that I saw them watch on television or in movies usually was rated G or PG or PG-13 at the worst. Films that contained sexual references, and propagated sensuality, nudity, profanity, and gory violence were an immediate no-no. Yet my parents did expose me to certain wholesome films that may have contained some violence or a bit of romance. They made sure to let me enjoy movies without being legalistic.

Despite the successes of my parents, they were still not perfect. Quarreling did not happen much, yet there was a time when my parents were involved in the greatest argument I'd ever witnessed with them. A marriage counseling session they were to have with someone had been canceled one evening—due in part to a leisure activity my dad had already planned—and my momma was not happy about it. Eventually, they got into a loud argument in their bedroom and my momma threatened to leave the house.

I was in tears, livid at my own parents, never having seen such hostility in them towards one another. Looking back on it, I don't think the fight itself was major. But I remember how isolated and targeted I felt seeing them yell at each other. It was the only time I ever saw them fight. This incident was a rare swaying from their usual behavior in contending for peace and love, qualities which I perceived and experienced from them all my life. My parents, just as any other couple, had their shortcomings.

When my family and I would eat out at restaurants, every once in a while my dad would take an opportunity to witness to the waitress or waiter attending us. I sometimes struggled with the fear of man as a kid, but being present while my father shared the Gospel encouraged me to be bolder. Also, his witness to others helped me see that he was the same man in real life as he was behind the pulpit. No hypocrisy existed.

One thing that you'll often see with carnal Christian parents is a subtle contradiction between what they profess and how they live. They will say to their children, "Do as I say, not as I do." Well, this is not the way I viewed things with my momma and daddy. They always demonstrated to me—by the power of their actions—what they believed. There was no beating around the bush. It was black and white. Holiness was exemplified and a desire to please the Heavenly Father was always of utmost importance. So, as a youngster, I emulated their lifestyle.

All that resounded in our house and in my ears was praise and worship music, words that glorified Jesus and transported me into the presence of God. Secular music never played. Lyrics that spoke scripture and underscored the goodness of Christ and his love continually resonated within our home, in our car, and of course at church meetings. Anything outside of that was foreign to me. Everything that my parents embodied, being ministers and people of God, was exemplified in their tangible living experience.

I am thankful to God that my parents were not legalistic, that they let me have fun, interact with other kids, and encouraged my gifts and talents. First and foremost, they let me play. I never experienced oppression from them and they never forced me into doing activities I was not passionate about. My parents wanted me to live out a joyous childhood, filled with unforgettable experiences. I was able to travel with them to West Africa and Europe, partaking in supernatural meetings and watching them as they ministered the Word of God and manifested the power of the Holy Ghost. Living examples, I admired them greatly and saw them as my greatest heroes due to their consecration to God.

Bert: If we as parents care to see our children walk with God, modeling our own relationship with God is an absolute must. We could be praying for our children to walk with God, but we need to understand that how we live our lives is a part of that prayer, and a part of God's plan.

They need to see and experience Christ in their midst. And how will they? God's plan is that they would see Christ in their midst through their parents, and through the influence of the Church. Unfortunately that's not always the case, as parents are not always walking with the Lord as they should, and the Church is not maturing sometimes as it should.

Ministers' children and especially pastors' children (not all ministers are pastors) often see the worst of the worst because they're around it. They see people go and people come. They see people complaining about this and that, being offended here and there. A close pastor friend of mine told me he believes the home of a pastor is not necessarily the best setting for raising children. That's an amazing thought, but it's true. They have challenges that other children do not face. Please remember that about your pastor's children, and do not put them on a pedestal.

Many pastors' kids have really, really struggled because they have seen beyond what other kids typically see. Be kind and understanding toward them. Other church kids see the pastor and the family, but they're not in the midst of it at the dining room table or the living room. They don't see their father go through the horrible circumstances of being accused of various things. It's tough. The reason I know this is because I have many pastor friends and I've been around ministry most of my adult life.

This is the reason I can say with utmost confidence that the greatest act of love we can offer our children is to walk with God, and put Him first in our life. There's no greater gift we could give our children.

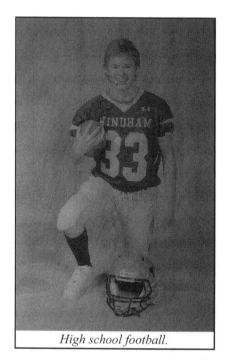

High school football.

High school baseball

Nice swing!

Chapter 7
Bond or Breach

"Shut up!" Those were the words a 10-year-old baseball teammate of Daniel uttered to his father under his breath from his shortstop position in the infield. Daniel, who was playing second base, overheard him and told me about it later. I used this opportunity to give my son another life lesson.

The father of Daniel's teammate was also the coach of the team. And he was yelling at his son for not doing something right.

There are certain indicators that act as symptoms of a relationship going sour. For a son to speak words like that to his father, even though unheard, reveals a breach in their relationship, that if not dealt with, will, with time, spiral out of control and greatly increase the risk of an irreparable and permanently severed father-son relationship.

Men are in prison today because of emotional imbalances and insecurities stemming from permanent breaches in their relationships with their fathers, or not having fathers at all. A recent statistic revealed that only 2% of imprisoned men have contact with their fathers as opposed to 98% who have contact with their mothers. Why is there such a sharp contrast in men's relationship to their fathers versus their mothers? The following passages of scripture will help our understanding.

"Husbands, love your wives [be affectionate and sympathetic with them] and do not be harsh or bitter or resentful toward them" (Col. 3:19, AMP).

"Fathers, do not provoke or irritate or fret your children [do not be hard on them or harass them], lest they become discouraged and

sullen and morose and feel inferior and frustrated [Do not break their spirit.]" (Col. 3:21, AMP).

Both of these passages are written to men. They reveal to us that men are prone to be more harsh and hard-hearted than women. For this reason, men generally do not laugh or cry as easily as women do, and they need to guard their emotions more carefully in this area of being bitter or hard-hearted.

Tenderheartedness is an attribute that men need to cultivate in their lives. For example, from the time my son was born I have hugged him and kissed him nearly every day I've been home. I have always endeavored to affirm my love for him and verbalize it every single day. When I make a mistake and am too hard or harsh toward him, either in word or in deed, I ask him to forgive me. These things create a bond between fathers and sons instead of a breach.

There are old men today who cannot say the words "I love you" to anyone or express the need to forgive or be forgiven because of the bitterness that has grown in their hearts over the years. This inability usually results in breaches in their relationships with their sons or daughters, relatives and friends. It is usually a reflection of their relationship with God as well. Men who cannot express the precious things that are in their hearts to those they love are not free.

I remember being at an ordination service years ago where many couples were being ordained into the ministry. Kenneth Hagin, a genuine prophet of God, and one of my spiritual fathers, was laying hands on them. Several times he admonished the husbands not to be so hard-hearted. Not once did he say that to any of the wives. Being newly married, this made a great impression on me. I made a determination not to be hard-hearted in my marriage, and I carried it over to my relationship with my son.

Having a son (or daughter) is like living with your heart outside of your body for the rest of your life. How are you treating your heart? Is it still like the feeling you had when your child was first born? Is he still your little baby even though he may now be a teenager or a grown man? Are there still warm, tender emotions that flow between you and your son every time you are together? If not, then perhaps forgiveness needs to be released and misunderstandings cleared so the breach can be repaired.

As of this writing, my son Daniel is 19 years old and a freshman in college. He is very tenderhearted, quick to forgive, and quick to repent. We can talk about anything. Trust is the fabric of our relationship, so nothing is hidden. To this day we enjoy a great bond that has been nurtured through the years, and I am convinced will remain unbroken throughout our lives.

As a father I certainly wish I could take back some moments of frustration with Daniel when I failed to display the fruit of the Spirit with him in my words or actions. For example, I have a very competitive nature. I can remember being at some of Daniel's ballgames and sporting events and displaying anger, disappointment, and frustration with Daniel, or even with the umpires or referees who were officiating the game. At times my wife did not even want to be with me as it was embarrassing for her, and for me—especially as a minister—to display some of the carnal behavior I did. Now I did not run out on the field and throw a temper tantrum and beat somebody up, but it was a problem about which the Lord convicted me strongly. My concern was not only that it didn't glorify God or was a poor witness, but what it was doing in Daniel.

One vivid moment that stands out to me was during a freshman basketball game. The time was running out in the first half and Daniel had the ball with a chance to shoot a last second shot, but he fumbled the ball around and couldn't get in position to get a shot off. I stood up in the stands and yelled out, "Shoot it!" But the anger and frustration that came out in my voice was unbecoming, and all the other parents heard me.

The one thing I will never forget, though, is the look that Daniel gave me. He gazed up at me in the stands and gave me a look of disgust and one of being publicly humiliated. That sort of scenario happened more than once. Knowing that this was an apparent weakness in me, I found myself apologizing to Daniel and being ever so conscious of giving him ten times more affirmation and encouragement than correction or even constructive criticism.

When I would pray and meditate on my behavior, I realized that the root of it was pride and a desire to have *me* look good. When children look good or perform well it makes the parents look good, too. It was more about me than Daniel. Certainly it is good to want your children to succeed at whatever they do, but we have to ask ourselves what the real reason is for our wanting their success. It's far more important who they are becoming than how they are performing.

God forbid that how your children perform in athletics and sporting events, or in any other field for that matter, should determine whether or not they receive approval and affirmation from you. That is a poor kind of fathering based on conditional love. This will create a breach in a father-son relationship very quickly.

Whether there is a bond or a breach in a father-son relationship depends more on the father. Breaches need to be repaired. Bonds need to be nurtured.

Fathers, are you doing it?

Daniel's Thoughts

I can remember when my 10-year-old teammate whispered those words, "Shut up!" to his father. It was sort of a shock to me. If it had been my father, I would never be able to say that. Transparency always formed the consistency in our bond. Like an open book, my dad would express his deepest feelings for me, and would talk about his own weaknesses and shortcomings. Therefore, I knew that my father was not perfect, yet in his imperfections and his willingness to share them, I held a higher respect for him. In turn, this produced a tighter bond because he wasn't just my father, but he became my friend.

A great factor that contributed to our close relationship was the amount of time my dad spent with me as a child. We would go to the ball field together, pray and worship together, watch sports together, and play pick-up games together. He was always around, a constant source of encouragement, support, and advice. Without him, I would have been left as a child to figure things out on my own.

I never felt anger or bitterness towards my father. There were times when I didn't always understand why he did certain things, and I became frustrated, and every once in a while emitted an attitude of disrespect and subtle dishonor. However, this never lasted for too long because I knew my father loved me and held my greatest interests in mind.

Filled with the joy of the Holy Spirit!

Color my world.

Chapter 8
Being a Wise Gatekeeper

"For in this trusted office were four chief gatekeepers; they were Levites. And they had charge over the chambers and treasuries of the house of God" (1 Chron. 9:26).

"Do you not know that you are the temple of God and that the Spirit of God dwells in you? If anyone defiles the temple of God, God will destroy him. For the temple of God is holy, which temple you are" (1 Cor. 3:16-17).

This chapter is a life and death chapter. Satan comes as a thief to steal, kill, and destroy (John 10:10). Whether the thief enters into your child's life or not is primarily dependent on the parents' gatekeeping skills.

What are gatekeepers? In 1 Chronicles 9, gatekeepers are listed by their names and various assignments. They stood at the entry points and the gates of the house of God. These gatekeepers had been appointed to a trusted office, and they carried great responsibilities to make sure nothing unholy entered in through the gates and nothing holy was taken out.

The house of God is no longer a building, but under the New Covenant our bodies are God's house or temple (Heb. 3:6). Our children are not mature enough to be the gatekeepers of their own house so we must fulfill that role until the time of their maturation. Our responsibility is to provide oversight in guarding and shielding their entry points from unholy access. The gates are the access points into your child's life: his eyes, his ears, his mind, his heart, his imaginations, his emotions, and his associations. Everything your child is surrounded by, especially in his early developmental years, is transmitting some kind of influence into his young tender life, either positive or negative.

Being a gatekeeper begins very early in life. The devil will even attempt to gain access to your child when he is still in the womb. As an example, when Carolyn was pregnant with Daniel, I sent her back to America from our residence in Gambia, West Africa. (Note: This was the second time I sent her back to America, the first being when she had the miscarriage.) The mortality rate for babies born in Gambia was very high, so we opted to have Carolyn deliver him stateside. She had planned to stay at her mother's townhouse in Michigan before and after giving birth, but during the pregnancy Carolyn received a dream from the Lord warning her not to stay there.

In the dream she was at her mom's house looking to hide some kind of treasure she had in her hand. Suddenly on the stairwell she saw an extremely large blob-like creature that filled the width and length of the entire stairwell. The word of the Lord then came to her saying: *"The spirit that possesses your mother will try and hurt your baby. Do not stay with your mother."* Carolyn's mother had been in an Indian cult for 30 years. In the dream she told Carolyn that this monstrous blob-like creature was her friend and would not harm her. The Lord told her differently.

Carolyn had no other place to stay and we didn't have money to rent an apartment, but we have learned that where the Lord guides, He always provides. Miraculously He opened up a house that Carolyn's brother owned and was now vacant. He allowed Carolyn to stay there rent-free before and after the pregnancy for approximately six months. We look back on that today and realize how big of a miracle that was because it spared the life of our precious son from being harmed or even killed.

If Carolyn had not been watchful perhaps she would not have heeded the Lord's warning. She could've easily dismissed the warning by reasoning it away with thoughts of no other place to stay. Gatekeepers are watchful over the lives of their children, even in the womb. We are not to watch in fear, anticipating the devil's schemes or plans. We don't worry or panic. That works against you and actually gives the devil access. But when the Lord warns us, or when we have no peace about a certain direction, we better pay attention to it.

There is a difference between paranoia and watchfulness. We are not to be devil conscious but God conscious. Do not fear, but receive the peace of God that comes from His wisdom.

Early in our children's lives, we need to develop an awareness of their surroundings and potential access points that could influence them in a very negative direction.

Television and the Internet

For example, television, and now also the Internet, are powerful influences on children. Since Daniel was a toddler, we have kept tabs on what he's viewed through the medium of television and the Internet. We would not allow anything of a sensual, worldly, or demonically suggestive nature to influence his heart and mind. Early in his childhood, if he happened to be at someone else's house, we would often inquire as to what activities were going on. Whenever television or videos were a part of the activities, we would inquire as to their content. Many Christians would not think of this as a big deal, but let me tell you that a lackadaisical attitude in this area displays great ignorance of the devil's devices (2 Cor. 2:11).

We have some good friends who are training their children this way, too. They have Christian relatives who also have children, but they are more lenient with them in this area. In one instance when all the children (cousins) of these two families were together watching a movie, there was a disagreement between the parents as to its content. Our friends didn't approve of the content while their relatives thought it was a non-issue.

The proof of the pudding is in the eating, as they say. In comparing the children of both of these families, it is clear as to who is more godly and sensitive to spiritual things.

Television and the Internet are transmitters. They are continually transmitting ideas, philosophies, patterns, concepts, attitudes, and spirits of one kind or another. Once the spirit of the world gets into your child, it will be difficult at a later age to uproot it because he's developed an appetite for it.

We consistently monitored what Daniel watched on television. He was not allowed to even turn the television on, or if it was already on, to change the channel without us being present. Often when we'd watch television with him, even the commercials were monitored. So many commercials today are very sensual and even demonic with subliminal messages. If anything suggestive or sensual came up on the screen, we were quick to turn the channel. Once we had conditioned Daniel to righteousness and exercised his senses to discern between good and evil, he began to do the same. As he grew we eventually allowed him to make some choices on his own regarding television.

Many of the producers and directors of film and television shows today are ungodly. There are atheists, gay activists, and new age gurus behind a lot of the programming. Compared to my childhood, it is appalling what can be viewed on prime time television today. The sexual innuendos, the language, the sensuality, and the humanistic nature of television programming today are alarming. Factor that in with the Internet content and you have a wide open door to every kind of lust, violence, and perversion. And people wonder why our society is in such a mess.

The media largely shapes the minds of any nation. God's Word commands us not to be conformed to this world's way of thinking, but to be transformed to God's will by the renewing of our minds. From an early age our children must know the difference between the world's ways and God's ways.

"And do not be conformed to this world, but be transformed by the renewing of your mind, that you may prove what is that good and acceptable and perfect will of God" (Rom 12:2).

Music

Music is another powerful influence in the lives of young people. At 12 years of age, Daniel came home from youth group one day and told me how his youth pastor found secular music on one kid's iPod. One mother of another teenager commented that it wasn't so bad to listen to secular music. Any parent who believes that is deceived. That mother did not understand the power and gravity of sin and how the devil gradually transmits it to our children. He uses transmitters such as television, the Internet, and music to sow seeds of corruption into our children's hearts and lives.

I am not saying that listening to a few secular songs is going to automatically corrupt your children. But once they acquire a taste and appetite for that kind of music, it will be like sliding down an icy hill. Usually there is no point of return. They will go from listening to what you may think is harmless music and songs to a harder form of secular music where sexual promiscuity, drugs, violence, and perversion are promoted.

Years ago my wife received a word from the Lord through a dream. The dream was a prophetic warning for a large church we were preaching in. In the dream she saw music coming out of a CD that was bringing devils into the church. Music has tremendous power to transmit that kind of influence.

Rap music is very popular in the younger generation today. At one point in high school, when Daniel was listening to it, I warned him. I asked him to listen carefully to the spirit of the music and to

93

tell me what he heard. Because sensitivity to God had already been cultivated in him, he got the point. There's an evil in some rap music that is very dark. Again, I'm not saying that form of music is all bad and can't be sanctified and used for God, but there's a beat in some of it that promotes evil. Be watchful.

Pornography

Due to the personal and private nature of this topic, I was not going to include a section on it. The longer I thought about it, however, the more I realized how large of a problem this is today in developing our sons' spirits and souls—and shaping a significant part of their manhood—the more I knew how necessary it was to address it. Every normal male will be challenged here. It is a part of the hormonal changes a man's body goes through and the sexual drive that accompanies it. I would be more concerned if a young teenager did not possess a sexual drive.

My first pastor once said that if you put a Bible and a Playboy magazine on a table in front of a healthy teenage boy, he will choose the magazine every time. That is how strong the sexual pull is at that age and on into adulthood.

When Daniel reached the age of puberty, I began to introduce the subject of sex to him slowly and gradually. I used a book by Dr. James Dobson as a guide to talk to him about the changes his body was going through. Daniel told me later that as a high school freshman, he saw an image of a naked woman—the first he'd ever seen. It sparked that sexual drive in him.

Pornography is everywhere today. It is literally at a teenager's fingertips. He can access it through his cell phone. Many are addicted to it and it drives them to promiscuity and to be sexually active at a young age. It can even create sexual deviates and lead to varied forms of perversion. In today's culture, homosexuality, as well as other forms of perversion, are spreading; these topics must also be addressed with your children at a pretty young age because our educational system is being flooded with gay propaganda, poisoning young children's minds.

I know the topic of sex is difficult for some fathers to discuss with their sons, but transparency will go a long way toward making your son realize that this is a normal part of life. You should ask the Lord for wisdom to address it; tell your son mainly that the sex drive is normal, that pornography and pre-marital sex is wrong, and how to overcome it. Still today I talk to Daniel frequently about it because it never goes away. It's always available and can always be a temptation. I keep him accountable and he tells me the truth. If he is struggling with it, he will usually tell me.

Having faced similar challenges myself as a normal warm-blooded male in this fallen world, I encourage him with compassion. The important thing is not to nag him about it in a way where it ministers shame and condemnation to him. Also, don't keep it hidden. The devil does not want it brought out in the open. He wants to keep it secretive and in the dark.

I know a mother who caught her teenage son masturbating, and it was so awkward to her that she didn't know how to address it. That's because it is not her responsibility to address it; it is the father's responsibility. Mothers cannot really understand a boy's sex drive like a father can. If you are a single mom, I encourage you to ask for God's grace and wisdom to address this topic with your son, or find a man you trust that could speak into him.

The father of this aforementioned teenage boy had not cultivated a real bond with his son so he was not comfortable addressing it either. Guess what happened? The boy walked around with a sense of guilt and shame for weeks and months at having been caught masturbating by his mother. The parents both told me about how abnormal he was behaving. I counseled and encouraged the father to open up to his son about it so he could be set free from that guilt and shame.

This is all I will say concerning this topic. Fathers, bring it out in the light and open it up for discussion. Be available for your son to talk to you about it. Tell him that you have gone through the challenges and temptations of it yourself, and that even now you are not exempt from it. There are materials and resources available out there that can help you. Use them if you need to.

Dating versus Courtship

Boys' constant exposure to pornography will likely lead to sexual promiscuity with girls. My wife and I do not even endorse dating. We believe courtship is the biblical model and standard. Again, there are many helpful resources available that teach courtship, so I'll be brief again here.

Biblical courtship is not a Christian substitute for dating. Christian dating is actually an oxymoron because their principles are polar opposites. Dating is the world's alternative to courtship and is based on "shopping around" until you find the right person. It is man-centered, self-gratifying, and dependent on the way the culture is going. It leads to anxiety, disappointment, broken-heartedness, sexual promiscuity, illegitimate children, abortion, as well as shame and guilt, not to mention the possibility of sexually transmitted diseases.

On the other hand, biblical courtship is unselfish, Christ-centered, and is based on accountability and getting to know one another even before the courtship begins. The purpose of courting is to determine if marriage is God's will for the specific couple. It is done at a respectful distance physically and emotionally so as to not hurt either person. Time is spent with one another in public, with parents and friends, or over the phone until a decision is reached as to the will of God for marriage.

You may think this is old-fashioned, but it is God's way. As a matter of fact, I personally do not even believe that premarital counseling is God's best. I would like to see more pastors and parents involved in a pre-engagement type of counseling. The purpose would be to further determine whether it is the will of God for a couple to even be engaged. It gives them one last opportunity to pull out of the relationship before an actual engagement.

Associations

The biggest transmitter in our children's lives may be this next one: associations. Yes, that's right! Your children's friends and peers, as well as other adults in their lives, can have a considerable impact on poisoning their young minds and polluting their pure hearts.

When Daniel played Little League baseball he made friends with a couple of his teammates. I watched them and noticed a certain degree of mischief in them—innocent in a way, as children often are, but potentially harmful in another. They were strong leaders and Daniel was, by nature and temperament, a follower at that time, although he's learned to be a leader since then. When the opportunity presented itself for the boys to hang out together, my wife and I made sure it was at our house and in our territory, where we could set the rules and boundaries. If not, these friends could potentially have influenced Daniel in a certain direction or introduced some aspect of ungodliness into his life.

Here's a tremendous scripture on how our children's associations could harm them:

"For the Lord has made the Jordan a boundary between us and you, you Reubenites and Gadites; you have no part in the Lord. So your children might make our children cease from fearing the Lord" (Josh. 22:25).

Children who have another spirit can cause your godly children to stop fearing the Lord. Until our children are strong enough to influence them for God, we need to be very watchful.

97

Here's an example. For several consecutive days when Daniel was still in kindergarten, we noticed a big change in his attitude. His kind and sweet disposition had become bestrewed with a subtle, sassy arrogance. We inquired of his attitude from his teachers. They reported that he was getting into sand-throwing, hair-pulling tussles with another girl, which was rather humorous to me. After all, he was only four years old. Our concern was with some phrases he'd picked up from other children that, when combined with the attitude with which they were being spoken, smelled of rebellion. It was foreign to Daniel's nature. Something unholy was attempting to gain entry. It was time to kick it out.

We spoke to him about his behavior with great tenderness as you would speak to a young child. But when we realized how much of an influence these associations had over Daniel at such a young age, we made a decision to pull him out and home school him instead. We wanted him, at this early stage of his development, to have a strong foundation in godly training in a caring environment from those who loved him most.

Some people may think that this is a little extreme. After all, we cannot isolate our children from the world they live in. And secondly, due to the varied situations, careers, and schedules of parents, not everyone is able to home school their children. This is a true and valid point of contention among some parents. To home school or not to home school created much discussion in our own marriage. Each of us must follow God's individual plan for our lives and our children. In our case, we were led of the Lord to home school Daniel during his elementary school years.

Actually, Carolyn had made up her mind that we would never put Daniel in the public school system. She had heard too many horror stories of Christian kids who had been tainted miserably and corrupted by the spirit of the world in public school. For some it is truly a gateway to hell. I, however, differed from her in this regard; I believed it didn't have to be that way. I was confident that God would give us wisdom to overcome the many casualties of Christian kids who were eaten up by the world in the public school system.

Although I understood Carolyn's point, I actually feared the other alternative more. I did not want Daniel to grow up not knowing how to relate to the world he lived in. I saw too many Christian kids who were this way; they were greatly intimidated by the world and not effective in relating to it without compromising their faith. Obviously there are many exceptions to this.

I knew that the key was in the training and the preparation we gave Daniel. We had to find the balance of preparing our son to live *in* the world without being *of* it. This is the greatest challenge for God-fearing parents who desire to raise their children in the true ways of the Lord. For Carolyn and me, the foundation of all our training was in our son having his own personal relationship with God. His parents' God had to become his own.

I had already decided that we would not isolate Daniel from the world, but instead we would send him into the world when he was ready. We prepared him in degrees and stages. First, we allowed him to play Little League sports (baseball and basketball). This way he would learn to interact with other children who did not have the same faith in God and values he did. The best part of that was it could all be done under our watchful eye. I arranged my ministry and travel schedule as best as I could to be at most of Daniel's games. And when I couldn't be there, Carolyn usually was.

Secondly, we allowed Daniel to play with neighborhood children, but again we kept a close eye on his associations. I remember peeking out the window one time and watching an older neighborhood kid bullying him out in the street. Immediately I walked out into the driveway and just glared at the kid. Soon he cowered down and changed his disposition. This presented another opportunity to teach Daniel to stand up for himself and never to be intimidated by any bully.

Turn the other cheek was not my lesson. That won't work with bullies. Now you may disagree with this, but I told Daniel in no uncertain terms that if anyone started a fight with him to make sure he finished it. I was not raising a coward. I was raising a champion.

Neglect in Gatekeeping

There are plenty of examples of parents who were careless gatekeepers and did not keep their children from evil associations and enticing environments. In time they suffered grave consequences. I know Christian parents whose children have strayed from God, are engaged in illicit sexual sin, are on drugs, or worse yet, have even left the faith and are now agnostics or professing atheists. This is an all too familiar story, even with good and godly parents.

Now please listen carefully to this statement: Godliness in parents does not automatically transmit to godliness in their children. Although I am a very strong proponent of the importance of the example we set in our homes and children's lives—and have even included an entire chapter in this book on the subject— without other factors this alone will not guarantee success in the training we give our children.

Parents can be godly while still falling short in neglecting their gatekeeping responsibilities. Adolescent children and young teenagers don't understand the consequences of yielding to certain temptations. We must be careful to shield them from such temptations, and set them up for success and not failure.

For example, teenage dating can lead to sexual activity very quickly. Today kids are having sex at 12 and 13 years of age. They are too young to understand the ramifications of that sort of ungodly behavior. I have godly friends whose teenage and college-age children have had babies out of wedlock, and their young daughters are raising those children today without a husband. In most circumstances, that's a hard life. But some were sexually active from a young age and developed an appetite for it. When young teenage boys and girls are left alone, the temptation is strong to engage in sexual activity. Before you know it, they are fornicating regularly without the parents' knowledge of it, and soon they realize the young girl is pregnant. Other times, the kids go off to college and mom and dad receive that dreaded phone call that their daughter is pregnant or their son got a young girl pregnant.

This is the reason it is so important that our children's hearts are established in grace and that their spiritual appetite is strong with the fear of the Lord as their anchor. Parents should guard against being so busy with work and life activities that they are not watching their children's associations and activities and keeping those gates to their lives closed. It is all too easy to become careless in our gatekeeping responsibilities as parents. Through your son's or daughter's associations, the gate to his or her heart and emotions can be opened to unholy influences.

The worst part of this is that parents don't often know until after the fact. Many are stunned and shocked when an unwanted pregnancy happens or when they find out their kids have a drug problem or, nowadays, are involved in homosexual or lesbian activity. Lives change quickly from these kinds of consequences. I have great compassion toward good, Christian parents and their children who have suffered through these things. It is not easy. Yes, God forgives, and through His amazing grace, He can totally restore and take what the devil meant for evil and bring much good out of it. But these parents, along with their young sons and daughters who are affected, often have to live with the consequences.

When some element of ungodliness is sown in the hearts of our children, it may go undetected for years and not show up until much later in their lives. Without godly instruction and correction from parents, coupled with godly sorrow and repentance in our children for acts of sin and rebellion, seeds of corruption will be difficult to uproot. Parents will often act surprised when their teenage or adult children exhibit certain fleshly or sinful behavior, but it didn't start there. It may take years for the fruit of the corruptible seeds sown in your child's heart to manifest, thus the reason for training them from a very young age.

Daniel's Thoughts

Although I was not conscious of how watchful my parents were over me, I don't remember ever having any exposure to carnal concepts and compromising ideologies. I didn't go to public school until my teenage years, so the experience of being with other kids who were raised in secular homes and without a real belief in Christ was unusual for me. When I did participate in Little League baseball and basketball, most of my peers possessed a natural innocence— which was to be expected at such a young age—so a majority of the time they did not influence me negatively.

As far as being gatekeepers over me, everything my parents did that I thought was hard or restricting at the time never produced anger in me or the belief that I was missing out. Because I was home schooled, I was not exposed to other children on a regular basis. I think that if I had been around unsaved kids, I would have experienced much more peer pressure to compromise my beliefs. Although this kept me from becoming like the world, many times I felt abnormal and incapable of relating to kids my age. This vast spiritual difference existing between children who did not know God and myself created a feeling of awkwardness within me. I had tendencies to be timid and have a fear of the world.

My identity was built in Christ alone. God-given and naturally tempered this way, at times I exuded shyness and passivity, especially around other kids. But I was also tough inside, and the lessons that my father had taught me about standing up for myself aided me well. However, I was not a natural-born leader; rather, I was given more to a compliant, teachable, and moldable disposition. I liked to relax, take it easy, and enjoy life. I believe I was also keen and possessed wisdom and insight from God (as my pre-birth prophecy so stated), and my parents catered their spiritual and natural training to my personality, particularly to how I responded to various forms of discipline and attitudes.

When I reached a particular age, due to the fear of man, speaking the Name of Jesus became difficult. There was evidence of a spirit of timidity, which my dad recognized and sought to root out. One Halloween evening, as parents with their children arrived at our front door asking for candy, saying "Trick or treat," we gave them candy. My dad took it a step further, though. He wanted me to speak the Name of Jesus to them as I gave them the candy. So he would have me say, "Jesus bless you" instead of just "God bless you." It helped me because I was afraid at first of what people would think, and how strange it sounded. Ultimately, it enabled me to overcome the fear of man, while at the same time establishing my identity in Christ and providing me comfort in His Name.

My father exposed me to the scripture Proverbs 28:1 to help grant me boldness when speaking to unbelievers. This poignant proverb declares, *"The wicked flee when no man pursues: but the righteous are bold as a lion."* This verse's use of a metaphor in comparing the righteous to a ferocious, headstrong mammal empowered my spirit and eventually allowed me to proclaim the Name of Jesus without embarrassment or shame.

As has already been stated in this book, the powerful seeds of spiritual training I received as a child reaped within me a deep and profound sense of good and evil, and carried over into my teenage years. For example, as my high school's senior prom neared in the spring, I still had not found a date and only two weeks separated me from the event. Due to my stand for Jesus and my reserved nature, I did not develop strong friendships with most girls in my school. Each of the girls I planned on asking to the prom had already been taken. However, there was one girl who I discovered did not have a date.

When I asked this girl to the prom, she said she'd go with me. Yet when the subject of dancing came up, she told me that she wanted to grind with me. Grinding is a form of dancing where guys and girls gyrate their bodies against each other, so it basically constitutes having sex with your clothes on. Since I had never been to a dance and was uncomfortable with grinding, I told her that I really didn't want to do that. I knew I would not have fun. I offered her the alternative of opting out if she didn't want to go with me. After a few days of letting her think about it, she chose to opt out. I think it was for the best because I knew that if I danced with her, my spirit would have bothered me the entire night.

As has already been said, my parents never allowed me to watch R-rated movies and they usually did not permit me to watch PG-13 movies. This, of course, was during my childhood. By my middle school and teenage years, they let me make more decisions on my own. In regard to music, they played praise and worship music which glorified Jesus. When we watched television together as a family, if a picture of a scantily clad woman appeared on the screen, my parents would normally turn the channel and say that the woman was being sensual. As an impressionable child, I naturally picked up on what my parents said, so, I would emulate them and comment that a woman was sensual whenever a half-naked female flashed across the television screen.

Unlike the stories of other church-grown kids, I never perceived attending services, or Christianity in general, as a religion or a have-to activity. In fact, my remembrance of actually being in church is not nearly as accurate or vivid as the time spent with my parents praying, reading the Bible, and worshipping God. As I said before, a majority of what I learned about God was gleaned from personal one-on-one time with my dad.

Playing in the leaves of Autumn in New England.

Bert and Daniel goofing.

Chapter 9
Cultivating His Spiritual Appetite

"Blessed are those who hunger and thirst for righteousness, for they shall be filled" (Matt. 5:6).

In my opinion, this is another very critical chapter. To me the truths in this chapter are vital to a child following the Spirit of God and godliness in his life. There is a very pronounced difference between behavior modification in a child and a child's heart being established in grace.

When children live with their parents, they often do things because they have to, but, once they leave home and external restraints are removed, they will do what they want. In other words, the heart is the internal compass of a child, and, as he develops and matures, he will always follow his strongest desires. Wise parents will be careful to feed his heart with godly desires, and through practice, have his senses trained to discern between good and evil (Heb. 5:14).

The responsibility of parents is to raise their children in such a way that their children will make godly choices from the heart. In order to make those right choices, they must learn the difference between their flesh and their spirits. They must realize the war that exists between flesh and spirit, and how the devil works through the flesh.

It is paramount that parents help to cultivate the ability in their children to move from external restraints to an internal motivation. Most children comply when parents are watching, but, if outside your presence they feel no internal restraint, you need to ask God for wisdom to help change that. To me, that is the greatest tragedy I see in parenting today—the inability to gradually move children from external controls to internal choices of the heart. This is the reason good kids will do horrible things. Often we think children have a spiritual foundation but later find out it was all external and only behavior modification.

I know of a dear couple whose son was raised in church, yet He returned from college one summer, after a period of living independently, and confessed to his parents his involvement with homosexuality. Both parents were shocked. How does something like that happen? Once the external boundaries of the home environment were removed, all that was left was what was in their son's heart. Apparently, in this instance, he didn't have enough of an internal foundation to resist this kind of ungodly behavior. In a moment of weakness and temptation, he gave the devil access through his flesh and unrenewed mind.

When one of my spiritual mentors was dying, during his final days on earth, he called one of his protégés to his side and asked him to watch over his only son, then 16. Here's what he whispered into his protégé's ear: "Johnny has been *around* the things of God all his life, but the things of God are not *in* him. Please keep an eye on him for me."

What a telling statement! This father had a pulse on his son's spiritual life. Unfortunately, this is the testimony of far too many church kids today. They are around the things of God, but the things of God are not in them. This chapter provides another key element so that this will not be the testimony of your own children. We want to help parents avoid this tragedy.

The spiritual appetite of your children determines the direction of their lives. In the natural, if your children go for days without an appetite for food, you would know that there is something terribly wrong with them. Why can't we be that sensible spiritually? If your children have no appetite for God, they are spiritually sick.

What do you say to good Christian parents whose son comes home as a homosexual? I didn't have answers for those parents, only compassion. He's still their beloved son. Christ-like parents are not going to forsake their children no matter what they do. They were late starters in training their children in God's ways. I do know that our God is a miracle working God and what seems impossible with men is possible with God (Mark 10:27). Through prayer and faith in God, as well as unconditional parental love, I know any damage done in our children's lives through the sowing of any corruptible seeds can be reversed. But as I stated earlier, prevention is always better and easier than cure.

This book's primary purpose is to help you raise your children from a young age so that things like homosexuality will be non-issues with them, because they will have developed such an appetite for godliness and a sensitivity to spiritual things that such behavior wouldn't even be a temptation for them. You can sow a multitude of good seeds into your children's lives, but one corruptible seed that is neglected and never uprooted, sown among all the good ones, is all it takes for the devil to begin gaining access into their minds.

As parents we did our best to train our son, Daniel, to follow his heart. His heart was a safe guide—only because the Lord had helped us shape his appetite with the Word of God so that he understood right from wrong, good from evil, flesh from spirit. Even when our son would sin and make wrong choices outside of our presence, his conscience was so tender that he would often tell us. That kind of honesty and transparency doesn't just happen.

A child has to be assured of his parents' unconditional love for him even when they disapprove of his actions. Trust has to be established. When children see hypocrisy in their parents' lives, trust will slowly erode. But if you speak openly about your own weaknesses to your children, they will develop more trust in you

109

and be unafraid to share their own weaknesses and shortcomings. This is one way to develop honesty and transparency with them.

Good gatekeepers keep a vigilant watch on their children's spiritual appetites. What do your children hunger for? What are they being fed? Do they have an appetite for the things of God? If they develop an appetite for the things of the world, it will be increasingly difficult to root that out of them as they grow older. Once they reach puberty and their hormones start changing, it will be much more difficult to reverse their appetites. This is the reason for training and shaping their appetite when they are very young and tender.

If children feed their flesh at the expense of feeding their spirits, it will show up in an apathy and indifference toward the things of God. If that apathy and indifference continue to grow in them, it will become a monster that will not die easily in their independent years when they will be faced with much more temptation and the freedom to do whatever they wish.

When we stopped home schooling Daniel and enrolled him in a Christian middle school, our eyes were further opened to the importance of shaping our children's spiritual appetites from a very young age. I saw so many church kids who had been around the things of God, yet most of them had no passion or fire for God. They just did what their parents told them to do out of duty, but their heart's desires were for the things of the world. I met some of the parents of these children, and I knew that outside of a miracle of grace, their double-standard would make it very difficult for their children to be true lovers of God.

For example, one day Daniel went to a middle school friend's house and saw that his parents had beer in their refrigerator and frequently drank it. By this time, he knew from our training and example that this was not the biblical standard. And yet, to keep our son from prejudging people and developing a legalistic mind-set we would often have to explain to him that not everyone was a product of good biblical teaching and training. This may have been the case with this boy's parents. Perhaps their church did not emphasize the Spirit-filled life and godly living. That is what we often had to do with Daniel because he began to see things he had never witnessed in our home or in the homes of our godly friends. Again, these all served as life lessons in his personal journey of spiritual growth and discovery, which continued throughout his school years and on into young adulthood.

From a very young age, we were very intentional about keeping Daniel around the presence of God and godly people. We purposed to cultivate an atmosphere of love and holiness in our home. Sounds and lyrics of faith-filled music were frequently heard in both our home and in our vehicles. Although at times Carolyn and I fussed and argued with one another as couples often do, our son never heard foul language. What he did hear regularly were words of apology and forgiveness.

As young parents we were far from perfect, but we knew we were given a holy stewardship to train our son in the ways of the Lord. We prayed with him and taught him to worship the Lord in spirit and in truth from a very young age. We taught him to respect and memorize the scriptures. We had him in Spirit-filled meetings. He was a part of prayer meetings in our home. We didn't depend on the church to provide the meat of his training and instruction in the ways of God. We knew that this was our sacred responsibility, and we took great delight and pleasure in it. He was not only our son, but our greatest disciple.

If God commands us to make disciples of all nations, how much more does He expect us to fulfill this mandate in our own children? It is shameful for ministers and saints to win the world while losing their own children.

In all Daniel's years of living with us, though witnessing our many imperfections, he could never deny that our lives were filled with a constant pursuit of Jesus and the will of God. All these things attributed to shaping his spiritual appetite.

In everything we did to nurture our son in the ways of the Lord, we were very careful to differentiate between religion and having a relationship with God. I will even go so far as to say that we went to extremes to protect him from religion. Religion is the exercise of certain spiritual rituals and practices without having a real, vital relationship with Jesus. A living relationship with the Lord breathes life and freshness into us while religion actually deadens and dulls us to the reality of His presence. We wanted our precious son to know just how personal God can be with His children. One such experience left another indelible mark on his spirit.

Daniel's Vision of Jesus:
When Jesus Becomes Real, Everything Changes

"I sat there a few days before my 10th birthday in the family living room, which was full of people. It was a Saturday night and everyone, including family and friends, were praying together. My mom was playing the keyboard and singing a song. I was sitting across from her on the other side of the living room, next to my dad, in a comfy, cushioned chair. As she sang, tears ran down my face. My eyes were closed. My heart was beating fast. I was immersed in a mixture of emotions as I shut out the world around me. I was literally at that moment seeing the face of Jesus.

My mom was singing about the glory of God, and there was something in those words she sang that I could not explain. I do not even remember the exact words. All I know is that they rang in my spirit over and over and over again. So I closed my eyes and began to worship my Creator. Then, as I continued to lift my hands in worship, the face of Jesus appeared to me. I was not seeing Him physically with my natural eyes; I was seeing Him spiritually with my spiritual eyes. His face shone like the sun, His hair glowed, and His countenance radiated with light. His eyes riveted me. They looked like two deep, never-ending pools of water.

I sat in utter awe. I was crying and trembling, with my whole body under the influence of what seemed like a heavy cloud coming over me. My dad, who was sitting next to me, turned to me and tried to get me to open my eyes. My attention was so fixated on the vision of Jesus that I did not open them but instead uttered something about the beauty of His glory. He asked me, "What's wrong, son?" Then I opened my eyes. The vision was over. I looked around me and saw all the people staring and smiling at me as they came to realize what had just happened. After the vision, I was still crying, and I was trembling with holy fear. I had felt the tangible presence of God in a way that has impacted my life forever."

Bert: Think of the implications of one encounter with the Lord like this and the mark it can leave on a young child. This was not our doing. All we did was create an atmosphere of worship. God did the rest. I cannot emphasize the importance of exposing your children to the presence of God. Religion kills. The reality of His presence is what brings life. When Jesus becomes real, everything changes.

Now some of you may disagree with me on this, but we were not overly strict with Daniel about church attendance. We knew to obey the scriptural admonition not to forsake the assembling of ourselves together (Heb. 10:25), but in our situation as ministers, we were in meetings quite frequently. For this reason, at times we would even take a few Sundays off each year from going to church services. This also served to demonstrate to our son that our salvation is not based on church attendance, but in simply living our lives for the Lord, endeavoring to fellowship with Him and being conscious of His presence every waking moment.

We did not want to over saturate our son with any religious practices that he might see as a substitute for a personal relationship with Jesus. If we're not careful, these practices can have an opposite, undesired effect on our children, and can actually embitter them later in life toward the things of God and inoculate them against the real presence of God. This is especially true in traditional churches where the presence of God is not manifested and miracles are not seen.

All of us, especially our children, must experience God's power and presence, and see miracles in the local church and in our homes and personal lives. It will prevent them from having any prolonged oppression and depression. It is recorded in the Psalms that when the people remembered the works of God in their tents, they rejoiced.

"The voice of rejoicing and salvation is in the tents of the righteous; the right hand of the Lord does valiantly" (Ps. 118:15).

But whenever they forgot God and His mighty works and miracles, they murmured.

"But soon they forgot his deeds...And they complained in their tents..." (Ps. 106:13, 25).

This simply means that whenever we see God openly and clearly manifest Himself, our memories themselves will serve as an antidote to the ills that seek to gain entrance into our lives. Expose your children to the power of God. Give them every opportunity to see miracles.

Other Defining Moments in Shaping His Spiritual Appetite

There are two aspects of the true Christian life that I feel are critical to our children's spiritual health. One is the love of God, and the other is the fear of the Lord, which we've already discussed. Children must know and understand the unconditional love of God and be grounded in it. They must know that God's love for them is not based on their performance and behavior. Secondly, they must

114

have a wholesome and reverential fear of the Lord. If parents do not exemplify these two attributes in their own lives and impart them to their children, it will be difficult for their children to develop a healthy spiritual appetite.

When Daniel was only three or four years of age I showed him a video of a dramatization of hell. This video featured several persons who had out of the body death experiences where they had a vision of hell. Some parents would probably not agree with showing extremely frightful scenes to such young children, but my intention was exactly that—to frighten him. I wanted the Lord to indelibly mark his spirit with visions of hell so that he would never forget it. The fear of the Lord is what keeps us from evil.

As we watched this video together I sat back and watched Daniel's expressions. His eyes were riveted to the television the entire time as vivid images of people descending into hell were playing before him. Just before the end of the video he turned to me in utter desperation and blurted out: *"Daddy, I don't want to go there!"* This was the beginning of his real salvation experience. I used the moment to minister to him and prayed with him to receive Jesus Christ as his personal Lord and Savior.

I've heard it said that children are the most impressionable between the ages of two and seven. Those are the greatest years of the shaping and development of their heart and soul.

Another defining moment happened when Daniel was nine years old and we took him to see the Mel Gibson production of the movie, *The Passion of the Christ.* Again, some parents thought the movie was too graphically violent and bloody for young children to see. We knew, however, that the impact upon our son would be notable and pronounced. At the end of the movie, before we even left the theatre, as viewers were still spellbound and in a state of deep reflection, I remember getting down on one knee under a strong anointing, and with tears, talking to Daniel about the overwhelming love of Jesus. This was all after he had witnessed the agony of the sufferings of Christ as it played out on the screen. These types of life-defining moments need to be taken advantage of and rehearsed with our children. My son and I continued to discuss this movie for weeks and months after we had viewed it.

Although it took years and an entire body of work to train Daniel in righteousness, there are certain life-defining moments that remain lodged in his memory. I believe these two experiences were pivotal in his development and in cultivating his spiritual appetite. These two experiences, along with the vision he had of Jesus that came afterwards, were very instrumental in shaping his spiritual appetite.

Just as positive experiences can serve to shape a child's spiritual appetite and catapult him into a fruitful future, unpleasant experiences can also deeply impact him in a negative direction. This is why we must be watchful to prevent or uproot any seeds of an experience that could damage a child's emotions at a very young age.

For example, I remember hearing the story of a nine-year-old girl who came home from school and found her mother in bed with another man. For a long time, that experience haunted her to the point where years later she could not consummate her own marriage with her husband. She was not able to perform sexually because that image would come up in her and stop her.

As we discussed in the previous chapter, it is extremely important we keep a watchful eye on our children. The devil could use one horrific experience to twist your child's personality and knock him off course for years to come or affect him for the rest of his life. I thank the Lord that the aforementioned young woman got help and deliverance; she is free today and enjoys a healthy marriage with children.

Evaluate your children's spiritual appetites. Inspect the fruit of your training.

If your children ever have a negative experience that you had no control over, use your authority in the name of Jesus Christ to rebuke and renounce any potential harm or damage that might otherwise have come from it. Speak to fear and put faith and courage back into them. Use any negative experiences to further instruct them and train them in godliness.

The following is a compelling journal entry Daniel wrote while still a freshman in high school. This served as another gauge that confirmed to us that the training we were giving him was indeed producing. He had secured his own relationship with Jesus and he possessed a healthy spiritual appetite.

Daniel's Journal Entry

Most people's dream is to get rich, be famous, or be successful and have a family. But my dream is that one day I will have the guts to lay down my life for the sake of Jesus Christ, my King. It's not the most popular life goal.

Today I experienced more dissatisfaction. What do I mean? I mean that we are dying spiritually. I long to get into the presence of God, but others are hindered by the natural realm. We are alive naturally, but slowly dying spiritually. I felt frustrated by something and I think it was because I have no desire for the natural things any more. All I want is Jesus to come alive in our churches and youth groups. All I want is the fullness of God in my life. Not games. Not movies. Not more entertainment to feed our flesh but more of the Word and prayer to feed our spirits. Let's finally die to our flesh, and come alive in our spirits.

Bert: At an age when most boys are engrossed in their video games and prone to being girl-crazy, it was refreshing to see a spiritual hunger in our son, a rarity in today's modern world. But it doesn't have to be rare if parents will carefully and consistently nurture the

117

spiritual appetites of their sons and daughters.

On the other hand, as parents Carolyn and I were also very normal people, not pseudo-saints. Our son witnessed my love for sports and a competitive fire and passion for winning. He recognized Carolyn's enchantment with movies and her fervor for fun. We did not ever want him to get the impression that real Christians were weird, insensible, or out of touch with earthly realities in any way. He needed to know that we were of sound mind and knew how to live and relate to this world without being of it. Often when we'd come across that brand of pseudo "Christianity," we'd have to give an explanation to Daniel that it was not normal.

Daniel: Overall, my dad placed the utmost importance on my spiritual life. He wanted to ensure that my foundation in God and that my relationship with Jesus Christ was rooted and grounded like a stalwart tree. Because of this, I was in church services all the time, on mission trips with my parents, always soaking in the presence of Jesus and the milk of the Word of God. It was always a spiritual experience.

There was this sense of deep, profound love, which I felt in those services. I was free to run, to dance, to sing my heart out to a God I knew—deep down—and who loved me unconditionally. Consciously, I couldn't tell you what was happening, but something jumped inside of me, a baby bomb of ecstasy, joy, and complete vulnerability and I felt that everything in the world would be all right.

All dressed up!

Chapter 10
The Stored-Up Mercy of God

This chapter is for those parents who have prodigal sons. I am hopeful that these words will encourage those of you whose sons (or daughters) started out serving in their Father's house, but who have since gone out and wasted their substance on sinful and riotous living.

This chapter is also for those parents who came to the Lord late in life without the opportunity to raise their children from the beginning in the fear and admonition of the Lord. There is hope for you. God is a covenant-keeping God and you can have a brand new start and believe for your children, even those who are now adults, to come under the blessing of God. Because of your decision to serve the Lord Jesus Christ, His mercy is now available to your entire household.

"For I, the Lord your God, am a jealous God, visiting the iniquity of the fathers upon the children to the third and fourth generations of those who hate Me, but showing mercy to thousands, to those who love Me and keep My commandments" (Exod. 20:5-6).

What a great responsibility fathers have to their children and ensuing generations! If we love the Lord and walk in obedience to Him, He will show mercy to our offspring even if they stray from God. What a promise!

David was one of Israel's great kings who understood the mercy of God. He had been a product of God's mercy himself. For example, in Psalm 51 he cries out to God for mercy in a prayer of repentance after committing adultery with a soldier's wife, and then having Uriah, the soldier, killed intentionally on the front lines of battle to cover up his act of adultery. No wonder David sang of the mercies of the Lord. He had been a great recipient of them.

"I will sing of the mercies of the Lord forever; with my mouth will I make known Your faithfulness to all generations. For I have said, Mercy shall be built up forever; Your faithfulness You shall establish in the very heavens" (Ps. 89:1-2).

Notice the expression, "Mercy shall be built up forever." Obedience and faithfulness to God actually stores up mercy for your children and your children's children, and successive generations in your family line.

Here is the promise God made to David.

"My mercy I will keep for him forever, and My covenant shall stand firm with him. His seed also I will make to endure forever, and his throne as the days of heaven. If his sons forsake My law and do not walk in My judgments, if they break My statutes and do not keep My commandments, then I will punish their transgression with the rod, and their iniquity with stripes. Nevertheless My loving-kindness I will not utterly take from him, nor allow My faithfulness to fail. My covenant I will not break, nor alter the word that has gone out of My lips. Once I have sworn by My holiness; I will not lie to David: His seed shall endure forever, and his throne as the sun before Me" (Ps. 89:28-36).

Even though David's sons would be punished for sin and disobedience, God said His mercy would not depart from David's seed, but would endure forever. God would correct David's sons without abandoning them.

David's son, Solomon, knew this well. He did not walk uprightly before the Lord as his father did, and although there were some consequences for Solomon's disobedience, the mercy of God was still effectual on his own son. Solomon put God in remembrance of his promise to his father David.

"O Lord God, do not turn away the face of Your anointed; remember the mercies of Your servant David" (2 Chron. 6:42).

"Therefore the Lord said to Solomon, 'Because you have done this, and have not kept My covenant and My statutes, which I have commanded you, I will surely tear the kingdom away from you and give it to your servant. Nevertheless I will not do it in your days, for the sake of your father David; I will tear it out of the hand of your son. However I will not tear away the whole kingdom; I will give one tribe to your son for the sake of My servant David, and for the sake of Jerusalem which I have chosen'" (1 Kings 11:11-13).

For the sake of David, who was now dead, God showed mercy to Solomon and his son. One righteous generation can store up mercy for the next generation and the ensuing generations to come. Our lives affect our seed even centuries from today. We must think beyond the here and now, and ponder the consequences of our disobedience to God and the rewards of those who fear Him.

"But the mercy and loving-kindness of the Lord are from everlasting to everlasting upon those who reverently and worshipfully fear Him, and His righteousness is to children's children" (Ps. 103:17, AMP).

"And His mercy is on those who fear Him from generation to generation" (Luke 1:50).

Our lives can be stepping stones or stumbling blocks for our children and future descendants. Every single parent, be it father or mother, whether they know it or not, are sowing seeds for the future of their children—either to produce good fruit or bad fruit, blessings or curses. Through a life of righteousness, you can build up and store up the mercies of God for generations to come. It doesn't matter if you come to the Lord late in life. It is never too late for the mercy of God. His mercy endures forever!

If you will serve the Lord and worship Him, He will make it difficult for your children to go to hell, or to not follow the Lord.

Some children who grow up in church, but then rebel in their teenage or young adult years, as the world gets their attention, will find it very difficult to be successful sinners. Why? Because too much mercy has been stored up for them through the righteous lives and prayers of their parents and ancestors.

Spiritual deposits of mercy and the blessings of God are credited to our account when we walk in righteousness and obedience to God. And these deposits can last for generations after we are gone.

For example, King Hezekiah lived several generations after David. He received a message from Sennacherib, the king of Assyria, stating that he would destroy him and his city. But on a certain night, God sent an angel to kill 185,000 Assyrians. Once again, God defended and saved the city for His and for David's sake.

"Therefore thus says the Lord concerning the king of Assyria: 'He shall not come into this city, nor shoot an arrow there, nor come before it with shield, nor build a siege mound against it. By the way that he came, by the same shall he return; and he shall not come into this city,' says the Lord. 'For I will defend this city, to save it for My own sake and for My servant David's sake'" (2 Kings 19:32-34).

This is absolutely amazing because David had been in the grave for more than 300 years—yet the stored-up mercies of the Lord were still in effect. Hezekiah had tapped into those mercies just as Solomon had done long before. Many people are walking in the stored-up mercies of God because of someone else's righteousness, someone else's obedience, someone else's prayers, and someone else's sacrifice. And they may not even know it.

The Word of God says that a good man leaves an inheritance to his children's children (Prov. 13:22). It is honorable to store up monetary blessings for our children and grandchildren, but how much greater it is to store up a spiritual inheritance and a supply of mercy for them.

It's not how you start the race, but how you finish that counts. David committed adultery and murder in his reign as king, but he poured his heart out before the Lord in sincere repentance. There were, however, consequences for his sin; the first child that Bathsheba bore him died, and the effects of his sin plagued his reign and his family for years to come (2 Sam. 12:10). But David continued to serve the Lord, and for his sake God remained faithful to the covenant that He made with him, and His mercy and loving-kindnesses remained on David'and his seed.

It never pays to sin, but it always pays to live for God all the days of your life.

My wife and I have served the Lord faithfully since our early 20s. We've had to repent of our sins and shortcomings many times, but we've never stopped pursuing His plan for our lives. For nine years we lived in impoverished nations of West Africa. It was such a joy to serve the Lord there—even with all the sacrifices we made. From the sometimes unbearable heat to the inconveniences of no electricity, gasoline shortages, and tropical diseases to two different civil wars that displaced us and plundered us of all our possessions, we have observed the faithfulness and mercy of God for many years.

Deep inside I've always known that there was stored-up mercy from our labor in those nations. We've seen God's blessings on our lives and affairs. We've been aware of operating more from a heavenly economy (Mark 10:29-30) than an earthly one. There is stored up mercy upon our son, Daniel, and if Jesus tarries, and he marries, that mercy will extend to our grandchildren as well.

"I remember your genuine faith, for you share the faith that first filled your grandmother Lois and your mother, Eunice. And I know that same faith continues strong in you" (2 Tim. 1:5).

Our God is a generational God. His will is for the perpetuation of our faith and godliness to extend to our descendants forever.

God will never forget our work and labor of love that we have shown toward His name in ministering to others (Heb. 6:10). He will never forget His covenant with us. His promises will never fail. If we serve Him, His goodness and mercy shall follow us all the days of our lives.

Faithfulness to God equals stored-up mercy for the present generation of our sons and daughters and those yet to come.

"But the mercy of the Lord is from everlasting to everlasting on those who fear Him, and His righteousness to children's children, to such as keep His covenant, and to those who remember His commandments to do them" (Ps. 103:17-18).

Daniel after a high school drama performance.

Take one.

Chapter 11
Painful Parental Wisdom

Parenting is not easy, especially in this superficial and technological age where deception is great, life so demanding, and distractions abound everywhere. Training your children in God's ways is very challenging. Many Christian parenting books can leave you with feelings of guilt and inadequacy. This certainly has not been the purpose of this book. As human beings we are all imperfect, and sometimes we need other influences from outside the home to help us figure it all out.

We all need help. We need the local church. We need mentors and fathers. We need to glean wisdom from those who have gone before us. We need to learn from their successes and failures.

It is not wise to make rash judgments against parents—as I did in my earlier years of immaturity when I'd see their wayward kids. I've matured quite a bit since then. No two children are alike. All have different temperaments and different levels of submission and pliability. Some have stronger wills than others. Yet I believe all of them can be shaped and molded into young disciples of the Lord.

Here are some testimonies from godly parents who had wayward children. This is their story, in their own words, of God's mercy and how they overcame. A couple of them are still in the fight. Their stories testify of the mercy of God and offer hope, wisdom, and encouragement for parents who are having similar struggles.

Parent #1

We raised our children in a good home and in good churches and Christian schools. Although our children had each made a profession of faith, been baptized, and churched, we realized as parents that we had not helped them develop their own personal relationship with the Lord the way we should have.

I would like to share with you God's delivering power for our son, Paul. After Paul got out of high school he began making really poor choices. He was married while living on the other side of the country. After he got married, he began to get involved with his wife's brothers. They introduced him to things he had not been involved with before. One thing led to another. He went from smoking pot to using other drugs. We did not know about the things he was involved with for several years. We spent a lot of time in prayer for our children, but when we found out about Paul we got on our knees and cried out to God for him. We bound and loosed every evil influence in his life. We prayed and declared the following scripture:

"And all your children shall be disciples—taught of the Lord [and obedient to His will]; and great shall be the peace and undisturbed composure of your children" (Isa. 54:13, AMP).

We took a stand for his life, declaring that as our firstborn son he belonged to the Lord. He would do better for a while and then become involved in drugs again. Due to the drug use, he and his wife divorced. Later he remarried and had two children. He just kept getting worse and worse as far as the drug use was concerned. Once again his lifestyle cost him another marriage and he was divorced for the second time.

God continued to protect him and keep him regardless of everything he was involved in. Three times he was pronounced dead and brought back to life. He was in two very serious vehicle accidents. In one of them he was on his motorcycle when a truck cut in front of him and clipped his motorcycle, and he was thrown off into the path of oncoming traffic. God spared his life, however, when he was supernaturally moved to the side of the road out of the line of traffic. Later he was in a truck accident and went through the windshield. That was the second time he was pronounced dead and brought back to life.

In 2004 Paul was wrongfully identified as a person working undercover by a dangerous group of people. He was kidnapped and almost lost his life. It was only through a series of miracles that God protected and spared his life again. Over the next few years, Paul experienced jail and prison several times. In those days he would recognize God's hand of protection on a daily basis.

Through everything our son went through, we refused to give up on him. We continued to pray for his protection and to believe God that he would be delivered from drugs and everything else he was involved in. My wife spent many sleepless nights in prayer. Through the course of everything we went through for years and years, I his father, had become bitter and resentful. God began to deal with me that I had to forgive and release him for all he had put us through. I had to ask God to forgive me of my bitterness and resentment. When I repented of my sin, shortly thereafter things began to turn around. Things did not happen overnight, but over the course of several years, Paul began to allow God to put his life back together. I once asked Paul, "Where did we go wrong? Where did we miss it with you?" He responded, "Dad, you didn't do anything wrong. You raised me right; I just made very poor choices."

Paul's life has completely turned around. He's been delivered from all he was involved in and has turned his life over to the Lord. He has a beautiful wife and is very happily married. He has a good job and they have purchased their own home. A restoration process has also begun with his children from his previous marriage. We are so proud of him.

We want to encourage any of you who have children who have not been saved or who have grown cold and gotten away from the

Lord. You just have to make the decision to stand on the Word of God and speak the Word of God over their lives. You must stand in the gap for them and intercede. You must refuse to give up. You must bind them to the will of God. God has a plan for their lives and they will fulfill the will of God.

Pastor Phil and Dianne Thurmond

Parent #2

I would've never said that I'm a man who is too concerned about what people think of me. But in moments when I've gone through something difficult with one of my children, one of the first things I had to deal with in my own heart was pride. I had to deal with thoughts of what people are going to think when they see this unfold. God helped me to see the motivation of my own heart. What was my biggest concern? Was my pure concern for my daughter, or were there mixed concerns? Where was I going to be in this whole mess? I'm thankful for those moments in my life. I'm so thankful how God has worked in my life and revealed the impurity of my own heart.

Going through an experience as a dad as I have with my daughter is very painful, because I love my daughter with all my heart. Now here's a different thought: Pain isn't necessarily your enemy. Of course, the enemy himself engineers pain to destroy us. But it's in moments of pain that we change. It's in moments of pain when we look at and reevaluate our lives. Many people come to Christ in a moment of pain. Many of us come to maturity in a moment of pain. It's that moment that reveals what's really in our hearts.

Moments of fear and other painful emotions like that can help us understand that we're really not anchored upon the Rock, as we should be. We're really not trusting the Lord, as we should be. I think life has a way of consistently opening our eyes and revealing what we're really trusting in, and what we're really pursuing in our lives.

What I've come to recognize, even in difficult moments with a daughter who's gone astray and gotten into sin and some real problems, is that she might not be listening to God during those moments of her life. She also might not be listening to me in those moments. That pain has caused me to get on my face in absolute desperation and empty my heart before God. God has brought me to a much, much deeper relationship with Him through these circumstances. My dependency upon Him is far, far greater than it used to be. I've become more and more aware of how little I can do sometimes in situations like that.

I've also learned that in many ways I could've perhaps enabled some of my daughter's behavior. If I hadn't bailed her out so many times, she could've matured quicker in certain areas and been more responsible. She's going through a very difficult time right now. She is living somewhere she'd rather not be. She'd rather be in her own apartment. She's finding it very difficult to be a single mother. She's finding it very difficult to make it with the kind of paycheck she gets every week. She's been very naïve. She says, "I can handle it. Everything's going to be fine," when people try to tell her that it's not going to be easy to raise a child by herself. "Oh, I can do it. I know I can do it! Everything is going to be fine. I'll have my own place. The baby and I are going to be fine," she says.

I could never teach her the wisdom she's learning right now. That's the real point I'm making—that I've learned to step out of it. I've learned to recognize God in difficult moments instead of just recognizing Him in great moments. In other words, there was a day when I felt that there was a better place for my daughter, so I took the responsibility to make sure she was removed from difficult situations by giving her money and provision. It's not that I was wrong as a dad by doing that, but what I didn't recognize is that it's in those difficult times that my daughter is going to learn.

It's a parent's natural inclination to protect and save their children from difficulties, but I came to the realization that I had to let go and let my daughter learn this the hard way. What I had to learn, especially in my latter years of parenting, was that I shouldn't be protecting my daughter from herself, and her challenges. In many difficult moments where I stepped in, I wonder if it might have been better if I hadn't stepped in. I wonder if I should've started this process of not stepping in and bailing her out when she was younger.

Even though parents may bring two, three, four or more children into the world from the same stock and the same house, they are all born with their own personalities. With multiple children a parent will deal with each one a little differently. With my daughter I've had different challenges to deal with than with my son.

So I've learned this: I should not try to relieve her of the pain of her mistakes. I could stand and agree with that old mentality of guilt that I am not a good parent if I do that. But no, I'm actually a much better parent by encouraging her in her pain.

God is not just dealing with my kids in their difficult moments, but He's dealing with me. And the reason He's dealing with me so deeply is because I'm inviting it. God is looking to develop me into the image of His Son, and He's going to use my daughter's circumstances to deal with me. I'm being transformed through this.

The Bible says that tribulation works patience. Being patient with your kids requires putting yourself in remembrance of how patient your parents were with you. It takes time to grow up. I want to see my kids walk with God. They've seen their parents walk with God. They've seen other people walk with God. I want to see them walk in places that I haven't walked. Remember that God is working in your children's lives. God is working in my daughter's life right now as she communicates with me in the middle of her frustrations. He's working in the midst of all that. He's made a promise to us as parents. He got a hold of our kids when they were young. They may have gone astray, but they're going to come back. And they're going to come back with their own personal revelation and encounter with Christ.

There's an old adage that says: When the student is ready, the teacher appears. Kids are not always ready to hear what you as a parent have to say to them until they actually go through something, and reality hits them in a moment of pain and difficulty when they need answers.

When I look at Jesus' life, do you know what I'm constantly receiving? He stayed in constant fellowship with His Father all the time. He was constantly listening to Him. He lived in that place that He's made available to you and me.

His disciples were being prepared for that even though they did not yet understand it at first. Jesus couldn't tell them everything because without the Holy Spirit, they were not able to bear it. They watched Him for three years. When they got filled with the Holy Spirit, it all came back to their remembrance, and they realized this: The Holy Spirit is a person and I can be led and guided by Him moment by moment. Well, how do I do it? The disciples did it by remembering how Jesus lived; they remembered the relationship He had with the Father.

That image of Jesus, during the three years the disciples spent with Him, was stamped on the inside of them. And here we get back to being parents, don't we? We get back to how important it is to be that image before them. The disciples couldn't understand yet, could they? Our kids may not understand at that point. So it's possible that even in raising our kids and modeling beautifully before them, they're not going to really understand why mom or dad are the way they are until suddenly the light comes on.

That light will come on somewhere at the end of the line; maybe it will be in college, or when they get married and have their own children. Sometimes, when they have their own children, they finally realize what an awesome job their parents did in raising them. They begin to see why their dad or mom were like this, why they were so protective, and always gave instruction. They've got to taste it.

Sin and disobedience can be a great teacher. You can't appreciate sin for what it is until you've been bitten by it.

(Author's Note: This father chose to remain anonymous in order to protect his daughter's privacy from any embarrassment or humiliation.)

Parent #3

Life doesn't always go the way you expect.

We raised our two sons going to church. Granted, we weren't saved until they were almost in their teens. And granted, the Protestant church we attended for most of their developmental years was not Spirit-filled or even Bible-believing, but we did what we knew to do to raise our kids in a supportive home and to live our lives for God. We were not perfect parents by any stretch, but we were committed to our family. We had no grid for what was ahead.

After hanging out with a stream of effeminate artist friends, it became apparent (though he was denying any attempt we made to discuss it) our youngest son was battling with same-sex attraction—and losing.

Within months of that realization, our oldest, who was living out on his own and working in a nearby city, broke the news to us that he was also living in a committed gay relationship.

In just a few short months our world and our dreams for our family's future came crashing down around us.

We spent the next full year reeling with grief and guilt. We repented over everything we could think of: our past sexual sins, critical judgments we'd made of those in the homosexual lifestyle, our anger issues, our busy lives, and the fact that we had come to the Lord so late in our children's lives. But mostly we ached. We worked through the shame, the confusion, and the sense of loss. We poured out our pain to only a few of our closest friends and our pastor.

We also grieved over the years that they had lived in shame and hiding, sure that they'd agonized for years, unable to speak with us about their struggle because we had been outspoken against the gay lifestyle. We had unknowingly been condemning our own sons.

You probably wonder how we could have missed it. I don't know the answer to that. But I'm sure they didn't want us to know, and I'm sure the part of us that might have seen it coming didn't want to know it either—or even to give life to our fears by speaking of them.

In the midst of it all, God took me deeper to a place where I didn't ache so much. He taught me about believing Him when in the natural it didn't look good at all. He gave me faith for this trial. Sometimes in the middle of the night, I'd get up to pray, as much for the relief of my pain as travailing for them. One of those nights God gave me a song with a chorus that pricks my heart every time I sing it: "He gave His Son for mine."

One Sunday He gave me a word in church, in the midst of our pastor praying. I heard a voice in my left ear, so real I turned my head to see who was there. It was the voice of God saying, "I will do that which I have purposed." I knew He spoke of rescuing our sons.

My husband came out of his quiet time one morning having heard God more clearly than he ever had. God said, "My plan to rescue the boys is love." God has pretty much repeated that theme all through this trial.

God is breaking our hearts for all those whom the enemy has

seduced with a lie of a mistaken identity. He's showing us His love for them. He's also taught us a lot about how, as His church, we have gotten it so wrong. We've tried to condemn into holiness—an approach more like the Pharisees than Jesus. God's way is to woo us with His love. I've been so convicted that it's only out of a revelation of His love that any of us choose to come to God and to serve Him.

There is a process in this, like any grief, I suppose. My husband and I still war in prayer for our boys' freedom, but we've learned to love them where they are. We've learned that love is really our only hope and His most effective tool. We've learned to be happy in today. There are situations that aren't what we signed up for. Sometimes we have to remind our kids of where we stand and set boundaries for what we'll allow in our home. But we've accepted them and their partners as part of our lives. They are our sons and always will be. Besides, we could never impact their lives in love if we lose our relationship with them! There is a point in our children's lives when choices belong to them, not us. As difficult as it is for us, this really isn't our decision anymore. It's between them and God.

Wayward kids aren't new to our generation and they're not new to God. He's taken time to encourage us and repeat Himself. He is willing and able to rescue our kids! I keep an index card file full of favorite scriptures; I call it my "war chest." I have tabs separating the topics for areas I tend to need to declare the Word of God over. The biggest section is the one with the promises of God for my kids. The best part of those promises is that over and over He says, "I will do...." Isaiah 49:24-25 says: *"Shall the prey be taken from the mighty, or the captives of the righteous be delivered? But thus says the LORD: 'Even the captives of the mighty shall be taken away, and the prey of the terrible be delivered; for I will contend with him who contends with you, and I will save your children.'"*

Isaiah 59:21 also says, *"As for Me,"* says the LORD, *"this is My covenant with them: My Spirit who is upon you, and My words which I have put in your mouth, shall not depart from your mouth, nor from the mouth of your descendants, nor from the mouth of your descendants' descendants," says the LORD, "from this time and forevermore."*

The first time I read that I wept. I was praying for my sons to be rescued and His response was a promise for all of my descendants forever! That's the covenant He makes with us!

Those scriptures and others stir my faith every time I read them. I war with them. I build myself up with them. God has been so faithful. We are learning to trust Him, to trust His Word, and to rest. That's what faith requires.

I wish I could tell you that the answers to our prayers have manifested. Not yet. But we stand in agreement with all of heaven, that He is able, that He is willing, and that our Abba Daddy is Granddaddy to our kids. His heart is clearly toward them.

God is still on the throne and we can still rejoice in the day He's made. And we are going to. He said that no one who trusts in Him will ever be put to shame (Rom. 10:11). In the natural it looks pretty messed up. But just you wait: *"As for me and my house, we will serve the Lord"* (Josh. 24:15).

And by the grace of God so will you and yours.

(These parents also chose to remain anonymous to protect their sons.)

Parent #4

This was not supposed to happen.

"Lord, I don't understand," I cried. "I know Ron and I aren't perfect parents, but neither are we hypocrites. Your Word says, *'Train up a child in the way he should go; and when he is old, he*

139

will not depart from it'" (Prov. 22:6).

I continued to plead my case.

"We have lived our faith, had our kids in church every time the doors were open, made Your Word the reference point for right and wrong, loved them unconditionally, and when we had to say no to something we found a spiritually healthy alternative. Why now, after 18 years of being in Christ has our daughter begun to question and challenge everything she's been taught, and everything we stand for?"

I sobbed until I had no strength left.

Suddenly the Holy Spirit whispered in my heart, "I never promised you she wouldn't be tempted. You need to pray that when she is tempted, she won't enter into it."

The Lord also reminded me that He is the perfect Father, and has problems with his children at times.

"Hear, O heavens, and give ear, O earth: for I have nourished and brought up children, and they have rebelled against me" (Isa. 1:2, KJV).

This began a prayer and spiritual warfare journey that lasted nine months until our daughter was restored to God.

If I had to retrace our steps, I would say the trouble began with an unsanctified relationship. In particular, a mother and her son came into our church, became born again, and seemed to grow spiritually for several months. Over time, the son and Mindy became friends; they attended some social functions together, and it became apparent that he was interested in her as a girlfriend.

I expressed my concern that he was a new convert and needed to grow and become stable and sound before she could consider anything beyond friendship. I made the effort to disciple him myself when he would come over for visits. I told her he needed mind renewal and some sanctification from worldly ideas. She wasn't having any of it. "I'm 18 and I can do what I want," was her response. So began the spiritual tug of war over many months that eventually culminated in her leaving home for three days. No, we didn't kick her out. I am not a believer in what some people call "tough love."

The prodigal son's father did not kick him out. The son's flesh seduced him, and he left of his own choosing. But from that moment the Father began by faith to fatten a calf that would be killed to celebrate the return of his lost son. He daily watched for him and expected him to return, and one day received the repentant one back into his home as a full son. The prodigal would have never considered going back to his father's house if he had been cut off.

When Mindy left home her father held her, cried, and begged her not to leave. I was weeping, but powerless in the natural to do anything. As she walked out the door, I watched as she almost collapsed on the sidewalk, yet continued to get in the boy's car and drive away. I knew nothing for certain, except that I had a covenant with God, and I was not going to let the devil have our daughter and her destiny.

"For we wrestle not against flesh and blood, but against principalities, against powers, against the rulers of the darkness of this world, against spiritual wickedness in high places" (Eph. 6:12, KJV).

For many months I had spent time daily lying on our daughter's bed, groaning and weeping in intercession, anointing her pillow and sheets with oil, declaring the Word and binding Satan's assignment against her. I believe the pressure became so strong in the Spirit that there had to be a yielding or a departure. This was not what I expected or wanted, but I was determined my baby would love and serve God.

I remember our Christmas tree stood bare in the corner of our living room for three days. My heart was broken. I just didn't have it in me to carry on traditions. I could feel depression trying to settle over me and heard the voice of the enemy in my ear, mocking me. I had to make a decision to go beyond my fear, hurt, and questions and press into God. I had to continue to "fight the good fight of faith." Giving up was not an option. My daughter's salvation and life were at stake.

Three days later Mindy called to see if she could come home. I assured her she was always welcome, that we never told her to leave. We had a talk with her and her friend. I told him in no uncertain terms the way things would continue to be while at our home. I told him I was aware of the mental seduction and psychology he was using on her to seduce her from her faith. I told him he didn't want to be in a war with me in the Spirit because I would win! Mindy was irritated, but nonetheless they complied.

Not too long after this her heart began to turn toward God. She was back in church, and their friendship was having problems. It began to unravel until finally he left.

I remember one particular service in worship when the Spirit of God came on Mindy, and she was delivered. The following week, in another service, she spontaneously took the microphone crying, and thanked everybody for praying for her, and said she had given her life totally to Jesus. The congregation was crying and clapping all at once.

The truth is that our children, although raised in a Christian home, still need their own encounter with God. He can't just be "the God of their fathers." He must be *their* God. That's why I always pray over the children of our congregation now, that they will not grow up "church kids" but be truly born again and know God for themselves.

In her bedroom Mindy wrote out a scripture verse and hung it on her wall. It read:

"Whither shall I go from your Spirit? Or whither shall I flee from Thy presence? If I ascend up into heaven, Thou art there: if I make my bed in hell, behold, Thou are there. If I take the wings of the morning, and dwell in the uttermost parts of the sea; even there shall Thy hand lead me, and Thy right hand shall hold me" (Ps. 139:7-10, KJV).

Today our daughter is happily married to our youth pastor, has two young boys she is raising up to be warriors for God, and she is helping lead our worship team as an anointed prophetic psalmist.

Obviously there's a lot of detail left out of this testimony, but I want to personally encourage every parent who has a child who is wayward from God. Don't ever give up on them. God's Word and His promises are true. When we pray, God can work. Know that as you intercede, speak the truth in love, fast, declare the Word over them, love them, train them, live it before them, that it's all having an effect.

"Thus saith the Lord; 'Refrain thy voice from weeping, and thine eyes from tears: for thy work shall be rewarded, saith the Lord; and they shall come again from the land of the enemy. And there is hope in thine end, saith the Lord, that thy children shall come again to their own border'" (Jer. 31:16-17, KJV).

Ron and Tammy Bacon

(Permission given by Mindy to share this testimony in the hopes it will encourage parents and help struggling young people.)

Daniel's first comp card for acting and modeling.

Comp card.

Proud Papa and son.

Proud grandparents with grandson.

The Graduate, 2013!

Chapter 12
Your Crown and Reward

"Behold, children are a heritage from the Lord, the fruit of the womb is a reward" (Ps. 127:3).

"Children's children are the crown of old men, and the glory of children is their father" (Prov. 17:6).

When children are conceived and birthed, they are a reward from the Lord, but when they begin producing godly fruit and manifesting honor and obedience as a result of your training, they become a crown. This is especially clear and evident in the third generation, when your children start training their own children.

On my 50th birthday my wife, Carolyn, planned a surprise birthday party for me. She even invited friends from out-of-state who flew in to honor me. They were secretly escorted to a back room and gave me birthday greetings via a microphone through a PA system. I had to identify the voice of each one. It so warmed my heart to hear their voices and to see them finally come walking out of that room to embrace me. It was all very touching until my own son, Daniel, spoke. Then I lost it and became unglued with overwhelming emotion as he recited a letter he had written.

Dear Daddy,

Thank you for all you've done in my life. You've made me and taught me everything I am and know. You've always been there for me to tell me the right thing to do or say. Without you I wouldn't know the things I know now. Without you I wouldn't have the boldness to look people in the eye. You've taught me to never be afraid or intimidated by anyone. You taught me that it's not about the dog in the fight but the fight in the dog. You've never doubted me. You've always encouraged me and lifted me up. You were hard on me sometimes, but it always helped me work harder.

You're not like most fathers. You always were able to spend time with me. You mentored me and you're a good example for me. You've set rules and boundaries in my life and it's helped me stay on the right path. Thank you for giving me the right mentors and teachers to help me in different areas of life. And I also thank you and honor you for living a consecrated and dedicated life to Jesus that does not compromise with the world.

You don't know much about technology, but you sure do know a lot about sports. You brought me up in sports and especially baseball. You gave me the chance to play my first year of baseball at eight and you've been working with me ever since. You've been the best Dad a son would want. You're tough and feisty, but you're also loving and caring. You're 5'8" on the outside, but on the inside you're a giant. Thank you for everything that you do and are.

I love you and happy 50th – 7-28-08

Daniel was 13 years old when he wrote this letter. Once he finished reading it, there weren't too many dry eyes in the house. A friend of mine told me later that he couldn't hold back the tears either. "That is all the affirmation you need," he said. In other words, the true validation of your life—and in my own case, ministry—is when your children honor and esteem you this way.

"*Discipline your son, and he will give you rest; he will give delight to your heart*" (Prov. 29:17).

That was a crowning moment in my life. I was beginning to see the fruit of our love and godly training being returned in honor. There was a peace and a delight in my heart. As parents, these are very touching moments that make us proud and thankful.

148

Leaving Home, Letting Go

When it was time for Daniel to leave home and go on to college it was a bittersweet time for Carolyn and me. Because of my temperament, believe it or not, I suffered more and it took me longer to adjust to his absence. After his high school graduation, I began relishing the remaining days we had left together. But Daniel did not share the same sentiments. He longed to be gone while I longed for him to stay. I was in the past. He was in the future. It was time to let go.

When your children reach their teenage years, they naturally become more independent, some a little sooner than others. This is normal, but hard on some parents, especially those who have a strong bond with their children. Here are some of the things you will probably begin to witness in your teenage children. They start becoming more private, spending less time with you, not willing to answer as many questions, wanting to be left alone—and boys not being as touchy-feely as perhaps they once allowed you to be with them, although that never stopped me from hugging and even kissing Daniel on the cheek nearly every day.

It was somewhat painful for me to see Daniel pulling away, though I knew it was a natural process of growing in his independence. The seasons were changing, and I knew it would never again be the same. This is the part I had to accept. Daniel was no longer the little boy who needed me in the same way he had in his earlier years.

Isn't it ironic that when your children are young they beg you to play with them and spend time with them, but parents are often hard-pressed to find that time due to the busyness of life? But then as they mature, it is the parent who longs for more time with them while they long for their independence. You've heard enough parents say it; enjoy them now for they'll soon be gone. You don't realize how true this is until that time comes upon you. It is a major adjustment for many parents.

Daniel was now a young man longing to spread his own wings and fly. The time was nearing for him to leave the nest. I had to accept this new season and not see it as a lack of honor or respect on Daniel's part. I gave him his space, and in my heart I began letting him go so he could grow.

At this juncture of his life, on his graduation day from high school, I wrote him another letter.

My Dear Precious Son,

This is letter #2; the first being at your birth.

Here we are at the end of another road on the journey of life. The first 18 years of your life have brought Momma and me great, and at times, unspeakable joy. We've watched you grow from a cherub-like tender sapling—so full of an intriguing curiosity and a melodious, harmonic disposition in such accord with the rhythm of life to a strong, independent, and ambitious young man, yet still seasoned with that same grace of earnest thought that savors so much of life and finds value in people of every diversity. In the words of the aged maestro: "An old soul" fits your description well —distinguishing marks for one so young as you are.

Today we celebrate this milestone with you—beholding not so much where you've been and what you've done, but who you are becoming. From the experienced perspective of our seasoned eyes, we are not celebrating the "day" as we are the "process." While reflecting back with gratitude and a sense of pride, we also look ahead with expectancy of the destiny for which God has called you. Leaving and entering is a large part of life and so you are leaving one phase of your young life and entering another. It is a moment in time, but one you will always remember.

You've done so well. Although Momma and I are very proud of all you've accomplished, we are most grateful for your love and fear of the Lord—evidence of the fulfillment of divine prophecy spoken over you even before you were in your mother's womb. From your childhood you've known the sacred scriptures, which shall continue to give you the wisdom and understanding necessary for your calling in Christ Jesus. Guard this trusted treasure with all your heart.

Life is full of pleasurable moments and crowning occasions—times of honor and celebration, such as is now. But life is also full of hardship and seemingly unfair situations that cause inescapable pain and suffering. In those difficult times, always remember the big picture. Step back and see those difficult moments in the light of eternity. Make big picture decisions—decisions based on your destiny, not on short-term emotions. This wisdom will serve you well and help you immeasurably throughout every season of your life.

We celebrate you today, son. As our only son, you have been to your mother and I sweetness, such that should ripen with time, like old wine. Our relationship, though the same as father and son, will be very different now in this new season of life and will continue to evolve with passing time. With college just a few weeks away, your bed and table seat will soon be empty, but our hearts shall remain full of the memories past while anticipating those yet to come.

We look forward with increased anticipation in sharing the joys of future earthly days and seasons while keeping our eyes permanently fixed on the eternal ages to come. It is our joy to release you with our blessing. Go and conquer and be all our bountiful Father has called you to be.

Congratulations, graduate!

We love you deeply and will soon miss you daily.

Daddy

6-14-13 – High School Graduation

Daniel's Thoughts: The First Few Months in College

When I first left for college, I thought of it as an opportunity for new experiences and my first shot at independence. I had never been away from home for an extended period of time. With great expectancy, I anticipated the chance to be on my own, to be responsible for myself, to be myself with people I didn't know.

Throughout my senior year of high school, I had undergone a steady change in my relationship with my parents. As the year progressed, I spent a lot more time alone than with my parents as I had done in my preceding high school years. With everything changing, there seemed to be a hint that nothing would ever quite be the same.

Spiritually speaking, my relationship with Jesus still held the highest importance in my life. I just sensed that I needed to be on my own in order for me to grow personally. In public high school, a social life for me was almost non-existent because most kids didn't share my values. Yet it had been a soul-searching process that involved the development of my character, my leadership, and my people skills. So as I entered college, my thoughts revolved around my social life, the people I would meet, and the friendships I would foster.

After being in college for about a month, there was a newfound sense of freedom in me. Though I communicated with my parents almost every day, I never saw them. Of course, I missed them and valued their support, yet I enjoyed the liberty of becoming my own person and making my own choices.

I can recall one Friday night in college when I experienced a slew of emotions when I thought about my parents. I returned from a school pep rally and was in my dorm room. As I lay on my bed, the thought of my parents entered my mind, and I turned on the song written by Keith Green, "Song for Josiah." Although I wasn't expecting it, a rush of emotions flooded me. Thoughts about my dad ran through me, and thoughts about one day having my own kids struck me.

I didn't know what hit me so strong, but I began to weep uncontrollably as I fell to the floor on my knees. I just remember thinking, "I want to be a better son to my parents. I want to honor them the way they should be honored." After everything that they had done for me and after all of the sacrifices they had made, I only desired to be half the son to them as they had been parents to me. Here are the lyrics to that song.

Keith Green's Lyrics to Song For Josiah

Oh my son, you were born in a world that hates you,

And I swear I will never forsake you.

But there was a father centuries ago,

Who watched his beloved son die. Oh, die.

Oh my son, I am weak and I'm trembling,

For the Lord I am always remembering.

Oh what a strong shepherd holds you in His arms.

He'll break you and make you His own.

And then take you home.

Well if I could I would protect you from what you will see.

This world will promise love and beauty, but it lied to me.

And I will show you, if you will listen.

And I will promise to listen, too.

Oh yes, there are some who love the lies,

they will kill you if they can.

Though you speak the truth in love,

they will hate you like the man,

Jesus, although he was God, he allowed himself broken for you.

Well if I could I would protect you from what you will see.

The world might seem so alive, but it's dead to me.

And I will teach you, if you will hear me.

And I will promise to hear you, too. Yes I do.

Oh my son, I am only your brother.

For a sister, God gave me your mother.

But just like a mother, so long ago,

had to watch her beloved son die,

Oh son, we will try, to let you go.

Bert: These lyrics written by Keith Green are a letter from a father to a son. While Daniel was home for Thanksgiving for the first time in more than three months, he burst into my study one night weeping uncontrollably. At first I thought something was terribly wrong, but then he embraced me, and through his tears, told me how much he loved me. He had been listening to this song again. I believe the lyrics opened up emotions of love and gratitude in him from seeing the season he was in from his father's perspective, and then imagining himself as a father.

When I listened to this beautiful song, that last line put a lump in my throat and tears in my eyes, too. I was in the midst of a season where I was learning to let my son go, and those words meant something.

A Longing for God

Daniel: A few weeks into my college experience, I found myself unable to sleep one night. It was 2:00 in the morning. An uneasy feeling gnawed at me in the pit of my stomach. I felt like I needed some type of relief from my unsettlement inside. I needed to experience a deeper spiritual satisfaction. I needed to be enraptured in the presence of Jesus. I needed to encounter the living God in actual experience.

So I got up, grabbed my iPhone and ear buds, turned on the album, "The Live Experience" by Keith Green, and took a walk around campus. For those not familiar with Keith Green, he was an extremely influential contemporary Christian artist in the late 1970s and early 80s. Green was radically saved and emerged as a follower of Jesus out of the hippie movement. Many of his songs on the album, "The Live Experience," recount his spiritual transformation and newfound love in Jesus Christ.

As I listened to his lyrics, just as I had done in times past, they penetrated me. His lyrics, pervaded with heart-searching reflections of his experience of being born again and becoming a child of God, conjured up longings within my own heart to know God more.

With shorts, a short-sleeved shirt, and flip-flops, I strolled through the campus courtyards and roads. At one point, I became so ecstatic about being saved that I sprinted several times around the campus' front circle. I felt like I was on top of the world. In fact, I was. I had undergone a renewal of the joy of my salvation. It's these times of refreshing that have always sustained my zeal for God and my hunger for righteousness even while being in college.

The Issue of Girls, Dating, and Partying

Throughout high school, I found myself extremely focused on my walk with God and my academics and extracurricular activities. I only had a few close friends because I did not compromise my convictions. Although I had a strong spiritual foundation, I still felt socially awkward mostly during my freshman and sophomore years.

Due to this self-consciousness, I was not completely at ease around girls. In general, I think I tried too hard to relate to my peers. Like many teenagers, I was in search of my social identity and comfort level. With that being said, I did not have an interest in dating girls. My parents didn't believe in worldly dating, especially with unbelievers, and I was too young. It would have only created an unnecessary distraction for me.

When I arrived at college, my initial mindset was on receiving an education, keeping my studies a priority, and undergoing musical training. I didn't want a relationship with a girl to become a distraction. However, little did I expect that one of my best friends in college would be a girl. We were in the same exact major and shared the same classes. As our friendship developed, she started developing feelings for me. I liked her and thought she was physically attractive. There was interest from me, but I did not want to rush into a relationship. Although she was a believer, she had not received the baptism of the Holy Spirit. This, of course, can only happen if the person has been born again and has a relationship with Jesus. As a real Christian, you need to be equally yoked spiritually with someone if there is even a possibility that that person is supposed to be your wife or husband.

This was my first time dealing with any kind of relationship, and I will admit that I became affectionate with her. It's difficult not to when two people are physically attracted to one another. I felt that we were spending way too much time together. We had only been friends since the beginning of the school year, and it felt as if we were in a serious relationship. The entire situation drained me emotionally as it did the girl. It was becoming a distraction from school and from my relationship with the Lord. Yet something in my spirit wanted to keep the friendship as I was having a positive effect on her spiritual life. So, we maintained the friendship and knew that we liked each other, but we both agreed to spend less time together alone and pursue the Lord individually.

In college, it's easy to spend time alone with a girl. However, if a guy and a girl spend a lot of time alone, they can become emotionally attached to one another very quickly. Even more importantly, becoming emotionally attached to a girl can keep you from pursuing God with all your heart. It could become a major distraction that may significantly hinder your relationship with Jesus and even cause unnecessary heartbreak down the road if the girl is not the one whom God has chosen for you as a wife. Don't fall in love with the wrong one! Proverbs 4:23 says, *"Above all else, guard your heart, for everything you do flows from it."* Also, when you are a freshman in college, it's not a good idea to start pursuing a serious relationship in which both the guy's heart and the girl's heart are involved. Both parties in a relationship must be seeking the Lord first and pursuing their callings, not pursuing each other.

Although I faced a real challenge with this relationship, I have not faced the temptation to drink or do drugs in college, for partying does not, in the least bit, interest me. Because I have the righteous nature of God, participating in sinful behavior like this is not desirable for me. Getting drunk or high is foreign to my nature, thus if I were to ever be intoxicated or high, the feeling of guilt and separation from God would sweep over me.

Returning Home

When I returned home for the first time since leaving for college, everything felt so strange. Initially, as I walked into my bedroom, I went into a state of near shock. I looked around my room. I couldn't believe that three months had passed since my last stay in this place. It seemed like ages ago that I slept in my own bed. Arriving back home hit me harder than what I had expected.

While other college students are able to visit their families once or twice a month because of their close proximity to home, I lived an 18-hour drive from my parents. They were in New Hampshire and I in Georgia. Thus, there existed both excitement and inner conflict in my brief transition back home.

I enjoyed being with my family again, yet I felt like I was trying to exist in two different worlds, one being home and the other being college. After the initial wave of conflict, however, I adjusted to being home with my parents. This was further proof that the seasons had definitely changed in my life, and would probably never be the same again.

Bert: Daniel was right. The seasons would never be the same again. When your son (or daughter) leaves home, everything changes for you and especially for them. Once they experience independent living, being home can seem very strange to them at first. They will still enjoy returning to visit, but most of them never again feel comfortable living permanently at home. I know it was that way for me many moons ago when I left for college. I was 18 and never looked back. Once I experienced the freedom of living on my own, I never had a desire to live at home again. It is that way for a majority of young adults. There may be exceptions, but they are not the norm, especially for young men.

As a father I had to make a serious adjustment in my thinking during this new season of life. I kept thinking when Daniel moved away to college that I was losing something that I would never regain or recapture again. I longed for the days of when he was still that little boy who needed his father in a much different way. I longed to hear all his questions to satisfy his curiosity, and for playthings he would bring me so we could play. I still longed to be that daily ear that would listen to his heart, and that daily affirming voice that would speak into his life. I longed to walk down to the ball field and throw batting practice to him, or shoot some hoops, or play catch with the football. I missed the frequent devotional times we shared, and the spiritual conversations we had. For the first few days he was in college, I kept thinking he would come walking through the front door, and it would be like old times. Perhaps these emotions were accentuated because he was our only son.

I was living in the past. I was trying to hang on to something that I thought I was losing. I needed a fresh, divine perspective of this new season. One day I was talking to Tim, a pastor and good friend of mine, who was in a similar situation. He had three children, and his oldest daughter was now a sophomore in college. He shared some sound wisdom with me concerning his own transition that encouraged me and gave me peace. Here's his story in his own words.

Grape Juice to Wine

We've always done everything together as a family. We've been careful to protect our children from feeling like the ministry is more important than they are. Even growing up, our kids had no desire to play with the kids next door; they were very content playing with each other. One of my favorite things to do is go on vacation as a family and just hang out together.

So, as the time approached for Sarah to go to college, I dreaded the day. It meant losing everything that meant everything to me. It meant our family life was over. Sarah would be gone and things would never be the same. And shortly thereafter, Gabie, our second daughter, would follow and then Zach. I felt like my life was being taken from me.

When they were little, we enjoyed such precious times with them. We often thought that we did not want them to grow up. When the kids were two, four, and six, it seemed so special that seeing them grow up to be 10, 12, 14 and then 14, 16, 18, we would be losing something. We came to find out that as much as we enjoyed them when they were really little, we also very much enjoyed them as they grew older. Things had changed, yes, but we were enjoying every season. When they were in their teenage years, we were having fun with them and enjoying them in ways that we

159

did not foresee when they were little.

With that as a background, dealing with the dread of our kids leaving home, I knew that somehow our lives would not be over, that God still had good days ahead of us that we would enjoy. But I could not comprehend that. Then He spoke to me:

"Your children are like wine. When they were young you enjoyed them one way. As they begin to leave the house, you are not losing what you had, that you valued so much. It is simply transitioning from grape juice to wine. It is the same fruit of the vine and you do not lose it. It just enters a new season where you enjoy it differently. And in the next season you will enjoy it more; it will only become sweeter with age."

Those words really helped me as I looked at the coming transition as losing something. Although I did not see how the future could be sweeter, I received that word and believed that I was losing nothing. In the new season I would enjoy my kids, not losing my family, but enjoying them in a more mature and sweeter way.

And so far, that has been my experience. It did not keep me from sobbing like a baby when Sarah left, but we did find it to be true in ways we could not then understand. Our little girl has grown from a teenager to a young woman. We have had the joy of watching her make this transition, becoming a godly woman, pursuing her future —the things God has for her, and we are very proud of her.

Our relationship has, in fact, transitioned with age. She is no longer the teenage girl who was very frustrating to deal with at times. No longer are we wrestling with how much we should tighten the reigns versus giving her liberty. Then it was a matter of trying not to lecture her too much, and stressing over how much she should heed our advice or outright discard it. Now she is the young woman who seeks our counsel, who wants our advice—and who misses being with us.

Now our insights are valued and we are missed. Our family dynamic has sweetened. All of our relationships are that much more precious. We are indeed enjoying this season like we enjoyed every other, and more.

Closing Thoughts

I quoted earlier in this book how someone once said that when you have a child it is like living with your heart outside of your body for the rest of your life. When Daniel was living at home, my heart was at peace. When he moved away to college and stopped coming home, my heart skipped a different beat. It had to adjust and more fully trust God with his life and future.

As long as your children are alive, waiting for them to come home will probably never change. Even when they become adults and marry and have their own children, there is always this longing in the parents for them to return to the home of their childhood or wherever you are. You know they can never stay for they have started their own family and home. Of course, this is the normal cycle of life and perfectly healthy and in God's design. Nevertheless, the longing in a true parent's heart to have them home and to be with them and their grandchildren never leaves. As long as you are on this earth with your children it will be so—in a way, your heart will continue to live outside your body.

Even when you leave this earth and are found among the cloud of witnesses in heaven (Heb. 12:1), your heart will still be longing for your children to arrive safely home on the shores of heaven, or in rare tragic cases, they arrive first and your heart is filled with hope to see them in eternity. This is also the heart of God the Father. Having lived with His only begotten Son from eternity past, He too had to let Him go on a mission far from home to a place called earth, to redeem its inhabitants with His very own life and precious blood.

In the fullness of time, the Son offered His body as atonement for the sins of mankind. On that old rugged cross, the Father remained silent as Jesus was separated from Him for the first time ever. Actually, the implication in scripture is that the Father turned His back on Jesus as He suffered an agonizing death on the cross. Yet the heart of the Father knew He would rise from the dead and return home to heaven to be reunited with Him forever. Likewise, there is a similarity in our journey as parents.

When Jesus, the only begotten Son, left heaven for earth, He continued to have fellowship with His Father, only in a different way, in a physical body. Even so, when the seasons change in a son or daughter's life and they leave home, you can still remain in fellowship with them and enjoy them in a different way.

Parents need to enjoy seeing their young adult children mature in responsibility and putting into practice all they've learned living at home under your supervision and guardianship. Enjoy watching them make their own decisions, and even learning from their mistakes. They will continue to grow and figure things out. But the real appreciation in their hearts for their parents, and the value they will have for all your godly training, will come when they start having their own children.

Then and only then will you also understand the glory that is in your children's children. Like aged wine, your legacy will grow sweeter and fuller with time. It pays to raise your children in the ways of the Lord. The honor and reward of it is beyond description.

Will there be trials? Yes, life is full of them. Will there be challenges? Of course! Even today we continue to trust the Lord with Daniel's life as he ventures out on his own so far from home. His college life has not been without challenges, but we trust his heart and the years of training he received at home. We trust his relationship with Jesus. Our hearts are at rest in knowing that he seeks God and listens to the Holy Spirit.

Fathers, your son (or daughter) is typically in your home for an average of 18-20 years before he ventures out independently to navigate his own little boat in this world's turbulent waters. Until then, with God's help, you, more than anyone else, have the greatest opportunity to shape him and mold him into the man he will eventually become. You've got one shot at being a father.

Make it count.

Daniel is currently pursuing his passion for music in his studies at college in Rome, Georgia.

Daniel in college.

ABOUT THE AUTHOR

Bert M. Farias, together with his wife Carolyn, graduates of Rhema Bible Training Center, founded Holy Fire Ministries in 1997 after serving for 9 years as missionaries in West Africa establishing nation-changing interdenominational Bible training centers with an organization called Living Word Missions.

From 1999-2003 Bert served as the internship coordinator on the senior leadership team of the Brownsville Revival School of Ministry and Fire School of Ministry in Pensacola, Florida, a school birthed from a massive heaven-sent revival that brought approximately four million visitors from around the world with an estimated 150,000 first time conversions. There Rev. Farias and his wife taught and mentored young men and women in the call of God and training them for the work of the ministry.

Bert is a missionary evangelist carrying a spirit of revival to the Church and the nations. An anointing of fire marks His ministry with frequent demonstrations of the Spirit and the power of God. With a divine commission to also write, Bert has authored several books with an emphasis on helping to restore the true spirit of Christianity in the Church and its leaders and preparing the saints for the glory of God, the harvest, and the soon return of the Lord.

Before being separated to the full time preaching and teaching ministry, Bert experienced a unique and powerful baptism of fire. His consuming passion is for human beings to come into a real and vibrant relationship with the Lord Jesus Christ through the power of the Holy Spirit and to become passionate workers in His kingdom thus preparing them for the second coming of Christ, being among the wise virgins and a part of the first-fruits harvest who will be received into glory and receive a sure reward.

Bert currently resides in Windham, New Hampshire with his beautiful wife Carolyn and sweet son of promise Daniel.

OTHER BOOKS BY BERT M. FARIAS

SOULISH LEADERSHIP

This book is for everyone…

- Who longs for purity of heart.

- Who desires to be set aright in the core of his being.

- Who dreads God's disapproval more than man's.

- Whose greatest phobia is the fear of a wasted life and burned-up works.

The works that endure the testing of God's holy fire will one day be rewarded. Others will suffer loss (1 Cor 3:12-15). Will your works stand the fire or will they go up in smoke?

In that day the motive of every heart will be made clear. Leaders will be judged by a higher standard. Only one question will matter then, and it's the same question that matters now: Are you building your kingdom or the kingdom of God?

THE REAL SPIRIT OF REVIVAL

In this book, Bert challenges the status quo of Christianity today and redefines its true spirit which is one of revival and of living the Spirit filled life. With one eye on the coming glory of the Lord and His soon return, and another eye on the harvest of souls yet to be reached, *The Real Spirit Of Revival* takes the reader into a preparation to becoming a true lover of Jesus and a passionate worker in His kingdom. These vital truths that dot each new chapter of this book are sure to awaken you as one from a deep sleep, and light a fire in your soul.

If you are tired of a mundane relationship with God and desire to burn with His holy fire this book is a must read.

THE REAL GOSPEL

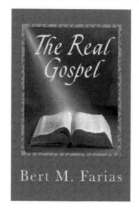

With piercing prophetic insight this book exposes the fallacies and shortcuts in the modern gospel and calls us back to Jesus and the cross. Its message reveals why so many Christians and churches today lack power, endurance, and character. Written in the spirit, style, and plainness of speech of the old timers, it breathes into today's shallow gospel the life of the spirit of holiness, giving us fresh eyes on old truths.

This is a critical book for the hour – a real wake up call to all. Backed by an abundance of scripture *The Real Gospel* is as truthful as it is radical.

THE REAL SALVATION

Can you imagine feeling secure in a salvation you don't even possess? Such is the state of mass humanity today. We have libraries full of sermons yet still so much confusion and deception about what the real salvation is. With poignancy and pinpoint clarity this short and sweet book cuts through the fat of satanic philosophy, exposes the deception of the broad way of religion, and shines the light on the narrow path to eternal life.

Most books are 200 pages with 30 pages worthwhile, and 170 of fluff. *The Real Salvation* is less than 60 pages, but every word counts. Make it count for you and your unsaved friends and loved ones!

PURITY OF HEART

The primary basis of all judgment concerning the deeds done in our bodies is our motives. Our values determine our motives, and our motives are the real reason behind our thoughts, words, and deeds. Only God can see the true motives of every man's heart.

Almost all human beings have something to hide. Nearly everyone twists words, events, and situations to their own advantage, to place themselves in the best possible light. Men often have ulterior motives and hidden agendas. This is sin and a form of hiding.

Adam and Eve first hid from the presence of the Lord in the garden after they had fallen. But there will be no hiding from the presence of the Lord on that solemn Day of Judgment.

Purity of Heart will prepare you for that day and spare you loss at the judgment seat of Christ so that you may receive your full reward. What is done in pure love, by the leading of the Spirit, and for the glory and honor of God shall reap the fullest rewards.

THE JOURNAL OF A JOURNEY TO HIS HOLINESS

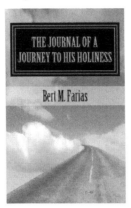

This journal-style book is not your normal run-of-the-mill literary work. Rather, it is a mystery from heaven unveiled---a saving word----a blueprint of the mind of God for every minister and saint. This journal will take you to a school beyond the veil wherein the Holy Spirit himself is the instructor.

The content of this journal reads like a tapestry woven by an unseen hand into the multi-colored fabric of each page. Its timeless truths and priceless principles will demand your prayerful attention; indeed a rare find for this day and age.

Don't just read this journal, but let it read you. Allow it to impregnate you with a depth of holy desire for intimacy and unbroken fellowship with the Father of spirits. There is a great purging and cleansing God wants to do in this hour in his Church, especially among ministers. This journal is one of those sign-posts that definitely point the way.

TO ORDER ANY OF THESE BOOKS
VISIT OUR WEBSITE www.holy-fire.org
OR AMAZON BOOKS.

MINISTRY INFORMATION

To become a monthly partner with Holy Fire
Ministries, schedule a speaking engagement or
parenting workshop with Bert and/or Daniel, or to
receive the ministry's free newsletter please contact:

Holy Fire Ministries

P. O. Box 4527

Windham, NH 03087

Web: www.holy-fire.org

Email: adm@holy-fire.org